GOOD·OLD·DAYS®

On the
HOME FRONT™

Edited by Ken & Janice Tate

On the Home Front

Copyright © 2009 DRG, Berne, Indiana 46711

Editors: Ken and Janice Tate
Managing Editor: Barb Sprunger
Editorial Assistant: Sara Meyer
Copy Supervisor: Michelle Beck
Copy Editors: Mary O'Donnell, Läna Schurb

Publishing Services Director: Brenda Gallmeyer
Art Director: Brad Snow
Assistant Art Director: Nick Pierce
Graphic Arts Supervisor: Ronda Bechinski
Production Artists: Nicole Gage, Janice Tate
Production Assistants: Marj Morgan, Judy Neuenschwander
Photography Supervisor: Tammy Christian
Photography: Matthew Owen
Photo Stylist: Tammy Steiner

Printed in China
First Printing: 2009
Library of Congress Number: 2008939412
ISBN: 978-1-59217-250-4

Good Old Days Customer Service: (800) 829-5865

DRGbooks.com
1 2 3 4 5 6 7 8 9

Dear Friends of the Good Old Days,

"Yesterday, December 7, 1941—a date which will live in infamy—the United States of America was suddenly and deliberately attacked by naval and air forces of the Empire of Japan."

With those words of introduction, intoned before the combined houses of Congress—and before the entire nation—President Franklin Delano Roosevelt issued a call to arms that immersed the United States in the great conflagration called World War II. It was in that crucible that this country's character was forged.

The next four years were a time of great privation. More than 400,000 military deaths in the various theaters of conflict were evidence of the supreme sacrifice. But there was another facet of the character that marked the "Greatest Generation."

On the Home Front, 131 million people mobilized to back the war effort. After we tearfully said our farewells to the men and women who would go into harm's way to preserve our liberty, we rolled up our sleeves and set to the task of making sure the troops were given everything they needed to carry our nation, the Allies and the world to victory.

Gasoline, oil, metal and rubber were in short supply, so it went first to Jeeps, tanks, bombers and ships. On the Home Front, we accepted gas rationing, 35 mile-per-hour speed limits and tires repaired so many times that we thought the patch glue was the only thing holding them together.

"Do With Less So They'll Have Enough" was the message from one World War II poster. Another proclaimed, "Be Patriotic, Sign Your Country's Pledge to Save Food." So, on the Home Front we learned how to make sugarless desserts and planted victory gardens to ensure our troops had enough to eat.

Fabric and clothing were rationed. "Use it up, wear it out, make it do, or do without." That was the catchphrase during the Great Depression, but it became more important than ever in the war years. Fabric for uniforms was needed on the front lines. Nylon was needed for parachutes, so ladies on the Home Front had to use leg makeup, or they simply went without hosiery.

The message to our troops was clear: "Your sacrifice on the battlefield will be honored by our sacrifice here at home. We will back you all the way to victory."

Where would our world have been without those who gave their youth, their strength, and all too often, their lives to pull the world back from the brink of tyranny? But where would they have been without us—the mothers and fathers, wives and sweethearts, younger brothers and sisters—who gave so much over here?

This book is dedicated to every person who ever licked a war savings stamp, used a ration coupon, riveted the seam on a battleship or plowed a victory garden. These stories belong to those who served in World War II on the Home Front.

Ken Tate

❧ Contents ❧

Over Here! • 6

For the Boys • 40

We Fought the War Too • 60

We Can Do It! • 94

Don't Sit Under the Apple Tree • 114

When Johnny Came Marching Home • 142

Over Here!

Chapter One

Farewells are never easy, and there were literally millions of farewells through the course of World War II. The "Greatest Generation" included, of course the brave men and women who bravely took the battle to the Axis powers "over there."

The song written by George M. Cohan for the doughboys of World War I continued to resound in the patriotic heart of America:

> *Over There, Over There*
> *Send the word, send the word,*
> *Over There*
> *That the Yanks are coming,*
> *The Yanks are coming,*
> *The drums rum tumming everywhere*
> *So prepare,*
> *Say a Prayer*
> *Send the word,*
> *Send the word to beware*
> *We'll be over, we're coming over.*
> *And we won't be back till it's over over there!*

But what about those of us who were left over here? Those of us who were too young or too old, those of us who were mothers, those of us too crucial to industry that supported the war effort also were part of that Greatest Generation.

We said farewell to our sons, daughters, brothers, sisters, husbands and fathers—and then put our noses to the grindstone and our shoulders to the wheel. Tearful goodbyes became faithful resolve to provide the support from the home front that our troops would need "over there."

In 1991, Good Old Days magazine published "Farewell, Young Men" by Marian Fredman, who wrote of those emotional partings:

Their parting words never reflected their real apprehensions.

"In the early 1940s, it was not unusual for members of our high school band, after being excused from class, to gather our instruments, and with teenage abandon, walk to our town's railroad station, where we lined up in parade formation at the side of the parking lot. Then, gung ho with patriotism, we played the usual American marches for our young men as they departed to serve their country in the Armed Forces.

"We watched mothers, sisters, young wives and sweethearts say their goodbyes. With tears streaming, they tried so hard to be brave. Their parting words never reflected their real apprehensions. Wives and sweethearts sent their men off with promises and dreams of their future together when they returned.

"Fathers and brothers bade farewell with masculine hugs, a thumping of backs and warm, meaningful handshakes. Heaven forbid that those brimming eyes let loose the flood as they spoke words of advice, encouragement and pride.

"We saw the Red Cross ladies, calmly and efficiently distributing coffee and doughnuts to the crowd. They never invaded the privacy of the farewells, but they were always ready if needed.

"Finally, the young men boarded the train amid waves and good wishes. As the train pulled out, we played *The Star Spangled Banner* with pride. Lost in thought, our walk back to school was slower and quieter. Farewell, young men! God be with you!"

The memories in this chapter are dedicated to those who bade farewell, to those who kept their hopes and dreams on hold for four long years, to those who served on the home front "Over Here."

—Ken Tate

Extra! Extra!

By Don Conrad

On Friday, Dec. 5, 1941, our family only had one radio, and it went bad. With the nation just coming out of the Depression, our family, like many others, could afford only one radio. Therefore, on that weekend, we turned to the *Middletown* (Ohio) *Journal*, the local newspaper that was delivered very early on Sunday mornings, for the news.

On Monday morning, I dressed, ate breakfast and left to walk the one and a half miles to McKinley Junior High for my eighth-grade classes. As I met classmates, they were talking about the attack on Pearl Harbor. I listened intently to learn what I had missed.

From all the conversations I heard, I pieced together the fact that the Japanese armed forces had bombed Pearl Harbor, a U.S. naval base in the Hawaiian Islands. What emotion should I feel? I wondered. Fear? Shock? Panic?

After the school bell rang for classes to come to order, my homeroom teacher gave a short dissertation on what had happened the day before. He prophesied that we would probably be at war shortly. He further suggested that our lives would change, and considerably so. When several students asked him questions, he replied, "What happens in the next several days will determine the answers to a lot of questions."

What emotion should I feel? I wondered. Fear? Shock? Panic?

In a later class, the teacher announced, "President Roosevelt will be addressing a joint session of Congress shortly. We will listen to it over the school intercom." Soon the normal popping and crackling of the system announced that something was coming forth.

Then President Roosevelt said: "Yesterday, December 7, 1941—a date which will live in infamy—the United States of America was suddenly and deliberately attacked by naval and air forces of the Empire of Japan." He continued speaking for some time, then brought his address to a close: "I ask that the Congress declare that since the unprovoked and dastardly attack by Japan on Sunday, December seventh, a state of war has existed between the United States and the Japanese Empire."

After the speech, silence lingered over the room until the usual popping and crackling signaled the end of the transmission. For the rest of the period, the teacher led a discussion on the importance of the speech. When the bell rang, all of us moved quietly from the room, unsure of what the future held.

One of our afternoon classes was interrupted by more popping and crackling from the intercom, followed by an announcement: "Any boy who wishes to sell extras can apply at 315 North Main Street after school." At the time, I did not have a job, so I decided to give it a try.

Like many families of the Depression, we found money scarce and telephones unnecessary. So, between classes, I called our next-door neighbor and asked her to tell Mom that I was going to sell extras after school.

After school, I walked the three quarters of a mile to the Main Street address. After a short interview and instructions, the manager gave me a cloth bag with a shoulder strap containing 40 *Kentucky Enquirers*. He suggested that I sell in the Upper Arlington area, which had prosperous families and very nice, large homes. Off I went, walking the mile and a half to the intersection of Sutphin Street and Linden Avenue.

When I got there, I held a paper in the air and shouted at the top of my lungs, "Extra! Extra! Read all about it! The Marines continue to hold Wake Island! Extra!" I repeated this as I walked up Linden Avenue.

A man came out onto his porch and yelled, "Boy, over here!" I immediately ran to him "How much?" he asked.

"Ten cents."

"OK, I'll take one." He held out the dime, and I handed him a paper.

I took another paper out of the bag and continued my trip up Linden. "Extra! Extra!"

I made several sales, and everyone seemed happy to get the paper. Some even offered me a nickel tip. And some handed me a quarter and said, "Keep the change."

After all the papers were sold, I went back to the Main Street office. "How did it go?" the manager inquired.

"It went good," I answered as I gave him his share of the money for the papers I had sold.

He then gave me 40 updated issues. The headlines on these proclaimed: "Japanese Continue Their Attacks on the American Bases in the Pacific." I headed back to the Upper Arlington area, but this time I went to Arlington Street. "Extra! Extra!" I yelled. "Japanese continue attack on Philippines! Read all about it!" Before I knew it, I had sold out again.

When I went back to Main Street to get more papers, the manager told me that it was 10 p.m.—too late to go out again. The time had flown. I gave him his money for the papers and headed home.

I walked the 2-plus miles home, where Mom fixed me a hot meal. She had no idea how much money I had made.

On Dec. 31, 2007, the *Columbus Dispatch* ran an article that stated that the last issue of the *Kentucky Enquirer* was being distributed that day. As I read it, a lump formed in my throat as I recalled that day I walked the streets of Middletown, Ohio, yelling, "Extra! Extra!" ❖

Newspapers for Sale! by Ron DelliColli, House of White Birches nostalgia archives

A Navy Blue Christmas

By Joyce Normandin

It was a cold and windy December Saturday in Brooklyn. Mom, my stepfather (whom we called "Dad"), my brother, Dennis, and I were out looking for our Christmas tree. We stopped at several tree vendors, but, as usual, Mom could not make up her mind. She was always looking for a perfect tree, and so far, none had met with her approval.

Dad noticed that my brother and I were starting to shiver in the cold, so he suggested that we take a break and stop in a little restaurant nearby on Seventh Avenue.

The restaurant was crowded. It seemed that everything was crowded in those days of World War II. We finally got a table in a corner booth and settled down. A waitress came to take our orders. Dennis and I asked for hot chocolates and muffins. Mom and Dad got steaming-hot cups of coffee and toast. I couldn't wait to warm my hands around that hot cup of chocolate!

They were young fellows, barely out of their teens, waiting for their ship to be repaired at the Brooklyn Navy Yard.

There were still a few customers waiting to be seated. Among them were two sailors bundled up in their navy blue coats. Their hats exposed their ears, which were bright red from the cold. Dad whispered to Mom, and then got up and approached the sailors. He asked them if they would like to join us at our table rather than wait. They shook his hand, nodded yes and followed him. As it was a corner table, we had ample room, especially when Dad sat Dennis on his lap.

They were just young fellows, barely out of their teens, waiting for their ship to be repaired at the Brooklyn Navy Yard, where Dad worked. Dan, tall and blond, was from a farming community in South Dakota. Steve, who had dark curly hair, was a little shorter. He was from Pittsburgh. The other guys in the Navy had nicknamed Steve "Smoky" because Pittsburgh was a very smoky city at that time. Steve asked me what grade I was in, and if I liked school. When I said I sometimes did but sometimes didn't, he laughed and said that was the way it was when he was in school.

When our orders arrived, Dad and Mom, and Steve and Dan talked and laughed while they ate. They seemed to enjoy themselves. It was clear that both Steve and Dan were pretty homesick. They mentioned how much they missed home cooking. When Mom asked if they would like to come home with us for supper, they both chorused, "Yes, thank you!" Dad explained that we were searching for a Christmas tree, and they seemed eager to join in the hunt. When we had finished eating, Dad grabbed the bill and paid for all of us. He said it was the very least he could do.

We left the restaurant with Steve and Dan in tow and marched along the avenue, stopping at a couple of places before Mom found her tree. Steve and Dan insisted on carrying it for us. We made quite a parade down the street—Mom and Dad in front, Steve and Dan carrying the Christmas tree, and Dennis and me bringing up the rear.

When we reached our apartment, the tree was put on the fire escape to stay cold until it was time to put it up and trim it. Mom started rattling pots and pans in the kitchen, and soon wonderful aromas filtered through the rooms. I had a Parcheesi set, and Dad, Steve and Dan set it up and played a couple of games with me. Then they settled down and started to discuss sports.

Mom served a very tasty supper; I think it was a meat loaf, as that could be stretched, with mashed potatoes, and carrots and peas. She had made a lemon pie for dessert and dipped into her rationed coffee to make a pot of coffee. Those Navy fellows really were hungry for home cooking, and they fell into the food with gusto.

Dan and Steve wanted to help clear the table and do the dishes, but Mom would not allow it. So I helped Mom, and the fellows followed Dad into the parlor and listened to the radio.

Soon it was time for them to leave. They took our phone number and address, and gave Mom and Dad their addresses. They then hugged Dennis and me, and left. We watched them disappear around the corner while we waved from the window.

On Christmas Eve day, we got a call from them. They had another short pass and wondered if they could visit us sometime over the holiday. Of course, they were invited to come right over and spend the night. They arrived with a carton of cigarettes for Dad and some

more coffee for Mom. We had a wonderful Christmas Eve. They helped us put up the tree and trim it. We ate and sang carols, and they attended midnight Mass with us.

On Christmas Day, they watched us open our presents. Mom had switched tags on a couple of presents and gave them each a small wrapped token. Then, after a breakfast of toast and scrambled eggs, Mom started to fix the turkey and stuffing for our dinner. Soon relatives started arriving, each carrying a dish. When someone said it looked like enough to feed the Army, Dad quipped, "Not the Army, the Navy!"

Steve and Dan left that evening. We didn't hear from them again for some time. Then we received a letter that told us they had shipped out soon after Christmas.

Those Navy fellows really were hungry for home cooking, and they fell into the food with gusto.

Steve could not say where they were, but he continued to write.

We had only one letter from Dan, thanking us for our hospitality. We never heard from him again. We learned later that he had been wounded and later died, which made me very sad. He was so young. Mom wrote a condolence letter to his parents.

Through the war years, our family kept up a correspondence with Steve. Even I would manage to send a few childish lines. Steve came through the war unscathed, but more mature, and he was not the same kid that he had been before. After the war, he visited us many times and brought his new bride, Susan. When their children were born, there would be a card and a present sent, and soon there would be a visit. Mom and Dad visited them too. They attended my wedding in 1956. They always stayed in touch. Then there were grandchildren.

It seems incredible that one chance meeting in a restaurant and an offer to share a table could result in a lifelong friendship. It continued for decades until, one by one, they passed away in the 1980s and 1990s.

Naturally, in time, everyone got older—even me! But I can still jog my memory and see those handsome young men in their navy blue uniforms, smiling and laughing as they helped trim our Christmas tree. ❖

A Vow to God

By Mary Lu Leon

In the window of my grandparents' farmhouse hung a flag with five blue stars. During World War II, five of their seven sons fought in the war. The oldest was based in Newfoundland; the next son served in the Philippines. The third son went to New Caledonia; the fourth, the only sailor in the bunch, saw action in the Pacific. The fifth was in Germany and witnessed the surrender of Germany. All these places, most of them previously unknown to us, occupied our conversations. We followed the war news with absorbed interest.

At age 7, I found the war frightening an absolutely all-pervasive. We had air-raid drills in our school basement. My cousins and I played blackout under the big oak kitchen table.

For an hour every night, my grandmother retired to her room to pray for her sons. Every morning she said a rosary before beginning the arduous farm tasks that women busied themselves with in the early 1940s.

"If they all come back safely, I'll crawl barefoot on my hands and knees up the church steps to give thanks to God," my grandmother vowed. Her words awed me. Even though I did not quite understand her proposed actions, somehow I sensed the important meaning behind her vow. On a farm, it was nearly impossible to keep one's feet clean, so the thought of her going barefoot to church amazed me.

Those who lived through that war remember how the main topic of conversation concerned the progress of the war. Each battle, each setback, each victory, made a difference in our lives. We saw newsreels of actual battle sites. Hollywood movies featured many stories about our Allied forces. We cheerfully accepted rationing of butter, meat, nylons and gasoline.

My grandmother fulfilled her vow. All five sons returned from the war. And she crawled on her hands and knees up the steps of St. Joseph's Church in Reedley, Calif., to thank God for returning her sons to the farm.

Only later, as I read of the washing of the disciples' feet by Jesus before his crucifixion, did I begin to understand the humility of exposing one's feet. My grandmother's example of faith and trust in God has stayed with me all my life. ❖

Five of the author's uncles served in World War II. They are (left to right) Toofeek, George, Sam, Pete and Joe Fagrey. Their mother prayed each day for their safety, and made a vow to God.

The Bombing of Terre Haute

By Phil Dunlap

Whenever the air-raid sirens went off, my head filled with visions of big, black German bombers overhead, preparing to plaster us good. I just knew that sooner or later, our town was going to finally get in on the action. Certainly a community the size and importance of Terre Haute, Ind., was a prime target.

I didn't know what role I would play, but I was ready nevertheless.

I was only 5 years old at the time, but the picture that I painted in my mind is still vivid. As almost anyone with young boys can tell you, 5-year-old boys live for action. If a boy should reach the age of 6 without a proper amount of action, one can expect some stunting of that child's sense of adventure, an important ingredient in adjusting to life's later challenges—like having children of their own.

At the first sound of a siren, Mother would scurry around, turning off light after light.

At the beginning of the war, my father was a volunteer air-raid warden, responsible for warning people to turn off all lights for a section of Terre Haute that covered several blocks, including the street on which we lived.

When those sirens sent their eerie wail bouncing off houses and apartment buildings all around us, Dad would rush to the hall closet and put on his steel helmet, a rather flat-looking, World War I style with a chin strap. It was painted white and had some sort of symbol on the front so that when he went to people's houses and told them to douse their lights or expect a summons, they would realize that he spoke with authority.

Sometimes I'd drag a chair to the closet where he kept that helmet so I could tug it off the shelf and try it on. I loved wearing it around the house, even though when I tilted my head just so, its weight almost toppled me over.

At the first sound of a siren, Mother would scurry around, turning off light after light. She pulled the dark drapes over the front windows so she could light some candles in case someone had to go to the bathroom while we were still in imminent danger of attack.

I preferred to go outside and watch the passing cars trying to negotiate the streets with no illumination but their parking lights. Not everyone took the potential for real danger seriously.

To make it easier for those doubters who just couldn't pull over until the all-clear sounded, the city had painted every tree trunk along the tree-lined streets with white paint from the ground to about 5 feet up. These white trunks made it possible for drivers to at least keep their cars between the trees, if not always precisely in their own lanes.

On one particular night, the radio reported that there was a huge fire at one of the factories near the river on First Street. We had to go and see for ourselves if the Germans had managed to plant a bomb down that old factory's smokestacks. I was certain we were under attack. The brick factory had an old Army tank parked out front on the wide lawn, and we figured they must make something inside that contributed to the war effort. That, of course, made it an ideal target for the devilish Nazis.

We had to drive slowly in my parents' 1939 Ford salesman's coupe, owing to the lack of lights, and also to my having to stand up in the back, clinging tightly to the back of the front seat. The salesman's coupe had no seat in back—just a big, empty area for a salesman to stash sample cases or whatever it was he sold.

We could see the reddish glow in the sky from several miles away since the city was blacked out. The flames shot high into the air as fire trucks pumped long spouts of water at the source of the blaze.

It was very exciting for a 5-year-old with an outlandish imagination.

Later, we found out that the fire had been

caused by an electrical short or something just as uninteresting. I really didn't care anymore what the cause was after it turned out to be just another old fire, and not the result of a sneaky enemy attack.

I was several years older before I began to question why we ever had those air-raid drills

A photo of the author in late 1942, prepared to do battle with the Germans in a uniform borrowed from his uncle, who was about to ship out with the Army Air Corps. He was sent to North Africa with a squadron of B-25 Mitchell bombers.

in the first place, since the Germans would have had to stop their planes for gasoline several times before reaching Terre Haute.

I couldn't quite picture German bomber pilots landing and buying gasoline in, say, Cleveland or Pittsburgh on their way to their intended target.

But then, when you're 5, *logic* is a word you haven't learned the meaning of yet. ❖

Hitching a Ride

By Audrey Corn

People don't stop much for hitchhikers anymore. But I remember a time, back in the 1940s, when folks trusted one another and life was simpler. This said, I still wonder whether Mama and Papa would have approved of a young girl like me riding in an automobile with that stranger we picked up along Route 17.

No matter; the decision wasn't mine to make. Uncle Ernie was at the wheel. He and I were driving to upstate New York to attend my cousin's birthday party.

I'd visited my cousin many times, and I'd pretty much memorized the way: Route 17 past Middletown, up through the Wurtsboro hills and on to our destination in Monticello. The trip ordinarily took more than two hours.

This journey, however, would not be ordinary. We were well out of New York City, but still more than an hour from Monticello, when Uncle Ernie braked to a sudden halt and began to back up along the shoulder.

A soldier wearing regulation khakis stood off to the side of Route 17, thumbing a ride. He lowered his arm and came running toward us. Uncle Ernie leaned across me and opened the front passenger door. "Climb into the back, Kiddo, and let the soldier-boy sit up front," he said. To the hitchhiker, he called out, "Hop in, son. Where you heading?"

"Ellenville, sir. It's still a long ways off, but I'd appreciate a lift as far as you're going."

"Ellenville, eh? Nice little town," Uncle Ernie said.

The soldier grinned. "My girl lives in Ellenville. I got a weekend pass, and hitchhiking is a lot quicker than riding the bus."

Uncle Ernie exchanged pleasantries with the soldier, but it was a hot July day—before the advent of air conditioning—and between the open car windows and the rattles of the old DeSoto, I couldn't hear what they said.

When we got to our turnoff, Uncle Ernie kept on going. What with weekend traffic and overheated cars, it took us forever to reach Ellenville. There was more unintelligible conversation between the two men. The young soldier must have been directing Uncle Ernie to his girlfriend's house, because a few minutes later, we pulled into the driveway of a small, well-kept white cottage.

A soldier wearing regulation khakis stood off to the side of Route 17, thumbing a ride.

In his eagerness to see his girl, our hitchhiker threw open the door and jumped out almost before Uncle braked to a stop.

"I'm much obliged to you, sir," the soldier said. "I just hope I didn't take you too far out of your way."

"Not at all," Uncle Ernie lied.

"Ellenville *is* out of our way. We're so late we probably missed the birthday cake," I complained when the hitchhiker had gone, and I'd reclaimed my rightful position up front.

"Kiddo, that young fellow is risking his life for this great nation of ours. I'm too old to serve on the front lines, but the least I can do is give a soldier a lift. Believe me, it was my pleasure."

We backtracked in silence along Route 17 and arrived 45 minutes late for my cousin's party. To my relief, they'd waited for us before cutting the cake.

When Grandma asked what kept us, Uncle Ernie mumbled some excuse about a detour. Nobody pressed him for more details.

Uncle Ernie didn't mention the hitchhiker that afternoon—or ever again—and neither did I. I understood that any reference to my uncle's good deed would only embarrass him.

Nevertheless, the experience stands out in my memory, one small example of the many unsung efforts on the home front during the Good Old Days. ❖

Children Fought the War Too!

By Jean Powis

Whenever I hear the wail of a siren in the dark of night, my thoughts go back to the days of World War II, when the piercing sound of an alarm meant that another air-raid blackout drill was in progress.

Home-front air-raid wardens had their tasks cut out for them as they banged on doors of homes and stores, yelling, "Lights off!" At the age of 10, it was scary for me.

Parents instructed their children to help turn off all lights when they heard the siren. Many times I'd complain because I had to sit in the dark with nothing to do. But my father always pacified me: "Be glad you're not a kid in another country that's being bombed."

Fortunately, American children never had to experience the direct effects of bombing or invasion, but they did participate in the war effort. Today's younger generation might think recycling is new, but we children of World War II know different. The kids in my neighborhood had "Help the War" clubs. Our mission was to gather masses of aluminum foil from cigarette and gum packages and any other place we could find it. We wrapped the shiny material into large balls, took it to our city hall and proudly received 50 cents a pound for our efforts.

We also helped bundle flattened tin cans from which we'd removed ends and labels, and we collected metal, newspapers and worn-out tires for reuse and recycling.

Shortages and rationing frustrated civilians. The scarcity of rubber left many children shivering with no boots. I had a big family, so boots (we called them "overshoes") were passed down to younger siblings and cousins.

When holes eventually broke through the rubber, we coped by putting heavy socks over our shoes before we pulled on the boots. We didn't mind because we knew we were helping our fighting soldiers.

It took me a while to understand what storekeepers meant by, "Don't you know there's a war on?" That was their reply to shoppers' complaints about the lack of sugar, butter and coffee on store shelves, and about the foul-tasting canned meat that largely replaced the fresh.

> *The kids in my neighborhood had "Help the War" clubs.*

Like adults, children learned to deal with the situation. I got used to home-baked cookies made with much less butter and sugar, and to the canned meat that we smothered with ketchup to disguise its taste.

Family backyards became the sites of "victory gardens" as Americans dug in to plant their own food and increase their productivity.

Sure, my friends and I grumbled when we had to weed and water the garden, but we had fun with it by having contests to see whose weed pile was highest, and who could grow the biggest vegetables. I won with my homegrown tomatoes and white radishes.

"Our soldiers need bandages," my grandmother told the girls in our family. She taught us how to knit simple bandages while she tackled socks. I missed my cousin Bob who had gone off to war, and I loved to send him letters, cards and boxes of homemade food overseas.

The war finally burned itself out and 1945 brought the end of four troubled years. Americans shared a bond of togetherness as they celebrated peace. As young as we were, we children had become home-front war heroes. ❖

"Here Comes the Mailman!"

By Artie H. Whitworth

It was 1944 in Wade, a small rural community in southern Oklahoma. It was the morning "gathering" at Uncle Bud's store and post office. (Uncle Bud was no kin to any of us; "Uncle" was just a pet name given to some of our elders.)

Over the years, the gatherings had been jubilant occasions, but now these were troubled times. Many of our menfolk were overseas fighting Germans and Japanese. We were in the midst of the awful World War II, which my Daddy said made World War I look like a scrimmage.

The mail carrier made his daily journey to our little town from the county seat. He would arrive about 9 a.m. when the weather was fitting. He would leave a sack of mail and pick up a sack that contained the community's carefully written letters on thin onionskin paper to loved ones in the war.

The tension began to rise when the sack was brought in and dumped on Uncle Bud's sorting table. His years of experience let him sort back certain letters to be given out at the very last.

First, he would pick out the onionskin (airmail) letters from the boys in the service and put them in the locked mailboxes with the little windows in the doors; or, if it was a general-delivery letter, he called out the name of the addressee. There would be squeals of delight from the wives, mothers and girlfriends of the letter writers, and after a silent once-over, the letter was usually read aloud so everyone could enjoy the news.

Many of the servicemen's letters had been cut up so by the American censors that it was hard to make much sense out of what was written. The men were not allowed to mention anything about the war effort or where they were fighting.

Several families had worked out a code system with their men, and using a coded map of the world on the living room wall, they knew right where their men were. Then, each night, they could listen to Gabriel Heatter or Walter Winchell on their arch-shaped Philco radio and know something of what their men were going through.

After all the other mail had been given out, the tension would again rise, for now would come the two kinds of letters that we all dreaded.

The first was a "Greetings from your Uncle Sam," telling the receiver that he was to report for examination and induction into the service. The age limit continued to be raised, taking more and more of our men. Though deferments could be requested for farming and other reasons, it was not considered patriotic in our community to do so, so no one applied for them.

The last mail included the letters that began with the dreaded words "We regret to inform you" and went on to speak of loved ones "missing in action," "taken prisoner" or "wounded in action." This was bad news for anxious mothers, wives and family. All of us were very sad because we were a community. Several of windows in our town displayed the stars that meant someone from the household had given his life fighting for our freedom.

Many who were at the gathering returned home with no news at all, but a deep sense of relief. But tomorrow we all would gather again at the post office to await the call, "Here comes the mailman!" ❖

> *Many who were at the gathering returned home with no news at all.*

The V-Mail Connection

By Miriam Biskin

During the Middle East crisis, when servicemen sent messages via e-mail, many of us were reminded of the days during World War II when mothers and wives, sisters and sweethearts awaited the postman's delivery with hope and trepidation. I recall the happy elation at the sight of a card or letter, and the disappointment when the man shrugged sadly with a "Nothing today."

The post office kept the human connection alive for everyone in times of crisis. Servicemen waited just as anxiously for every mail call to receive those loving words from home, and department statistics tell us that more mail was shipped overseas then than at any other time in U.S. history, with recorded sales of over $1 million in money orders and more than $100 million in postage stamps.

In an effort to expedite service and provide more cargo space for war materials, the postal department inaugurated V-Mail service, and in the months between June 1942 and November 1945, processed 1.25 billion pieces of microfilmed correspondence. The name *V-Mail* was suggested by a postal employee; it was an adaptation of Prime Minister Winston Churchill's famed "V for Victory" morale-boosting slogan. The official inscription included three dots and a dash (Morse code for *V*) after the letter.

The postal department had studied the process for some time before the war. A similar service

Left: A V-Mail letter from the author's husband.

was already in use between London and Cairo, and between Canada and England through an agreement with the British Airgraph Co. and Eastman Kodak. After some negotiation, our war, navy and post office departments contracted with Kodak for the microfilming and processing of correspondence.

Soon, every American family was familiar with the single 8½ x 11-inch sheets of thin paper. We all took care to write on one side of the paper only and to avoid the margins. The sheet could then be folded into an envelope that bore a bright red ¼-inch line along the top edge with an address box on the face. On the reverse were instructions for usage.

Servicemen's messages were accepted without payment, while civilians paid 3 cents for regular domestic service and 6 cents for airmail. The stationery itself was free to the public and servicemen in limited quantities, and private firms were allowed to reproduce the sheets for sale.

Although the post office received many requests for permission to use V-Mail for advertisements, circulars, etc., V-Mail was reserved for correspondence.

Some of us felt that photographed reproductions were too impersonal. We couldn't send snapshots or clippings from the hometown newspapers by this means, and the only photographs sent were those of infants born while the servicemen were overseas or who were under 1 year of age. And if, by chance, the correspondent was careless in writing or used pale ink, the reproductions were illegible.

An unbelievable average of 1,500 letters could be reproduced on one roll of film and

World War II poster, House of White Birches nostalgia archives

reduced to 3.15 percent of their original volume and weight. For example, 100,000 letters after microfilming weighed only 30 pounds as opposed to 1,000 pounds of regular mail. V-Mail stations were then set up in New York, Chicago and San Francisco, where letters were sorted according to destination and microfilmed. This film was then shipped by mail to the overseas destination provided with reproducing units.

To assure delivery, the original films were filed, and in the event of accident or loss, they could be reprocessed and redispatched. Best of all, service was better and speedier. By and large, just finding one of those pale blue red-bordered letters in the mail was a definite morale booster. ❖

The War Came Home

By Ellen B. Fredericks

*I*n the fall of 1941, I spent every weekend in San Pedro Harbor on Hank Roger's sailboat. We had a regular crew of three, and all of us worked in defense industries. Hank was an engineer at Douglas Aircraft; Ken was with Pratt & Whitney engines; and I was a secretary at Lockheed. So we certainly knew there was a war in Europe, but it seemed far from San Pedro.

Our slip was the last one on a long dock filled with pleasure boats. We were directly across from the U.S. Coast Guard station, close enough so we had a "waving acquaintance" with several of the Coast Guardsmen.

There was a lot of work to be done on the boat, so we spent every Saturday sanding, varnishing, scraping and doing maintenance chores. Sundays, we usually sailed around inside the harbor. None of us knew too much about sailing, and one day we even becalmed ourselves by sailing into the lee of a huge tanker. Gradually we learned, however, and one lovely weekend in late October, we decided to take the big step and sail over to Catalina.

Suddenly, the searchlight stopped— and it was shining directly on us.

Early Saturday morning, we chugged down the channel and sneaked around the end of the rock breakwater. In the open sea, we hoisted the sails and pointed for Catalina. It was a beautiful blue-sky day, and the wind was just right. The sun was warm. A school of porpoises even showed up to dive and leap and play beside us. Without a worry in the world, we lolled around the cockpit, drank a little beer and soaked up a lot of sun. We made the isthmus with no trouble and dropped anchor in the harbor there overnight.

Sunday morning, there was a party with some people from a nearby boat. We were later than we planned in starting back to San Pedro. The wind quit about halfway across, so we had to go under power. By the time we approached the mainland, it was pitch dark.

Anchored outside the harbor entrance, right in the center, was a boat with a powerful searchlight revolving atop its bridge. It meant nothing to us. We never sailed after dark, and for all we knew, it was out there every night.

Then, suddenly, the searchlight stopped, and it was shining directly on us. We all stood up and waved. The light resumed its movement shortly, and we continued toward our breakwater.

Soon it stopped on us again. We waved again. This happened several times.

Then, as we came closer to the breakwater, the boat started shooting off red rockets. We watched, fascinated by the fireworks, till Hank said, "You know they're shooting those things in our direction. Maybe we better go over and see what they want." We changed course and headed their way. The rockets stopped and the light started revolving again.

Photograph © 2009 by Robin Tate

When we pulled alongside, the boat turned out to be a Coast Guard cutter. An officer asked where we had been, and when we had left the harbor. On learning that we had sailed out the previous morning, he informed us that since our departure, the entire harbor entrance had been surface-mined, except for a small channel between two buoys at the center. If we did not go between those buoys, we risked being blown up.

We sailed in safely, a little shaken by our close call, muttering to each other about how dangerous it was for them to do such a fool thing. Everybody sneaked around that breakwater. We thought we had better tell all our friends about this! We never wondered why they did it. We were too naïve. War was something in the newspapers that only happened to other people.

Six weeks later, after our usual Sunday boat-breakfast, we set about our chores. I was sanding the rail, and a portable radio in the cockpit played *Old Black Magic*. The mast swayed easily against the pale blue of the sky. Across the channel, a couple of our Coast Guard friends leaned on the rail of their boat.

The music stopped, and an announcer's voice cut in: "Pearl Harbor is under attack by the Japanese Air Force!"

We were mesmerized, but not our friends in the Coast Guard. Over there, men were running. We had never seen so much activity. Within minutes, they had guns mounted on the boats. One by one, each cutter blew its whistle, three times in an ascending scale, "bleep-bleep-bleep," and quickly headed down the channel into the main part of L.A. harbor.

All day, like the rest of the country, we were glued to the radio. I still remember our frustration and disgust when the news was regularly interrupted by a commercial. "Does your tickle-tickle-tickle make you cough-cough-cough?"

By the time we left the boat around 5 o'clock, the L.A. harbor was surrounded by soldiers. We were stopped for identification three times, by soldiers bearing rifles and bayonets. They told us we could not return to the harbor without special clearance and I.D. papers that would be issued only to official crew members as specified by the boat owner. We were told that all the Japanese in the harbor area were being picked up and put on Terminal Island.

The war was no longer just in the newspapers or happening to other people. It had come home. There was a reason for those surface mines. ❖

My Armband

By Lynne Watkins

It seems a much lighter subject now than it was back when World War II was in progress. Our lives, our daily events, changed drastically! Our quiet little Pennsylvania mining towns changed, as did the situations in large cities. Nothing—and no one—remained the same. But those of us left at home did what we could to protect our country and our lifestyle.

Although I don't recall hearing the term "air-raid warden," I joined in their meetings, and somehow I became the chief air-raid warden in our little town. I acquired a colorful red, white and blue armband, and I wore it proudly.

We attended all the meetings to learn what we could do to help in case of emergency. We took first-aid classes and advanced first aid. It all seemed surreal at the time, but we learned every day how to be prepared.

Some very serious meetings were held at the local high school. We sat on the bottom bleachers and listened, aghast, as instructors advised us about mustard gas and other critical possibilities. I shuddered. This is America, I thought. This could never happen here!

Without warning, we would hear our local air-raid sirens blow. Immediately, we would take to our posts, patrolling streets. After dusk, we had to see that everything was dark. Blinds had to be pulled down tight so that no light shone through.

In our own home, Mother and Daddy were both ill, and we did not have all the necessities required. Using pieces of old, cast-off, dark green blinds, we tried to repair our damaged blinds to make them reach. But the glue dried and cracked, so we used black thread to stitch the pieces together to make the blinds extend all the way to the bottom. A few were in such bad shape that we just had to keep them closed all day to protect and salvage them.

If someone's blinds weren't drawn after the sirens blasted away, we were authorized to notify them at once. One dear friend and neighbor simply refused to be caught up in the new rules. He often worked the night shift, but occasionally he was home. I had a choice: I could ignore it, or I could obey orders. But I could not ignore it! I told him we would have to report it unless he cooperated.

When that didn't faze him, that's just what I had to do. I didn't hesitate, but I worried that our family would lose a dear friend. With both of my parents ill, if he came home from work late at night and saw a light on in our kitchen, he would stop in to see if they needed help.

However, he remained a kind friend of my parents. And after that, he did draw his blinds and follow all the rules.

At the meetings, I learned about so many things that could happen in the United States. We grew to understand why it was so necessary to have our boys and girls over there, fighting to keep our homeland safe.

My husband did come home from the war, following hospitalization. My sister's son, however, was killed in Korea, and my cousin was killed on Leyte Island.

I still have my wartime armband tucked away among my souvenirs. When I recall those meetings when I thought, *This is America; this could never happen here*, my thoughts turn immediately to Sept. 11, 2001.

I know now how important it was to do all the things we did in preparation for any disaster, to protect our beloved United States. Preparation is so necessary, and we must go to all lengths to continue to keep America safe. ❖

> *We sat on the bleachers and listened, aghast, as instructors advised us about mustard gas.*

"Air-Raid Warning Yellow!"

By Peggy McClain Frailey

"Air-raid warning yellow!" Those words meant that an air-raid drill was under way, as part of America's home-front defense plan during World War II. I was about 9 years old when my hometown of Mount Union, Pa., conducted its first "blackout," or nighttime drill, in the spring of 1942. The federal government had determined that the Eastern Seaboard, including Pennsylvania, was vulnerable to enemy attack and needed to be on the alert.

These blackouts were both exciting and scary for us kids. My 12-year-old sister, Nancy, and I would pull down all the blinds in the house, close the curtains as tightly as we could, and turn off all the lights. Outside, streetlights were extinguished and storefronts darkened. All traffic was stopped.

These blackouts were both exciting and scary for us kids.

My dad was an air-raid warden, so at the first signal, he would grab his helmet and armband, and rush out of the house to his post. My sister, my mother and I would sit in the dark in the living room and wait out the drill, which could run anywhere from 15 minutes to half an hour. It seemed like an eternity.

My imagination worked overtime during those darkened minutes. I crawled under a coffee table, hoping it would protect me from any bombs the Nazis might drop on our house.

We knew it was only a practice drill, but it seemed very real to us. And our imaginations raised all kinds of questions: "What if this is the real thing? Is our dad all right out there in the dark, maybe facing German soldiers?"

We strained our ears, listening for the drone of airplanes like those we saw and heard on the Movietone News at the movie theater—or, God forbid, for the blast of bombs being dropped. My two brothers were in the Army, and the younger one was overseas, so I can only guess at the fears these drills must have caused my mother.

It was always a relief when the all-clear signal came through. We could turn on the lights, open the curtains and blinds, go out onto the front porch and watch the streetlights come on again.

Mount Union was a small brickworks town in south central Pennsylvania, located along the Juniata River in Huntingdon County, off Route 22. The town was strategic to the state's defense production.

Brickworks at both ends of town turned out bricks for the kilns of the big steel plants that engaged in defense production. The Pennsylvania Railroad's main line ran through town before crossing the Juniata to the east, between Mount Union and Kistler, and an automobile bridge spanned the river between Route 22 and the north end of town. A small airport lay on the outskirts.

There were several documented "sightings" of spies and saboteurs in our area. A woman who worked in the library was

The author circa 1942 in the backyard of her home.

interviewed by the FBI after reporting that a stranger had come into the library and looked at maps and photos of bridges. When photographs of a group of captured German saboteurs appeared in the newspaper, a local schoolboy recognized one as a man he had seen leaning against a house, sketching something while he studied the nearby railroad overpass near the middle of town.

During the practice drills, the local air-raid wardens stood guard at the bridges and airport, and at all the local intersections and entrances into town. These wardens became "certified" after special training, and they had the authority to enforce all the blackout regulations.

My dad, Fred McClain, was appointed chief air-raid warden for Huntingdon County

in the fall of 1942, and civil defense became a focal point in our home life. We kids were very patriotic and took a lot of pride in helping the war effort. My father appointed my friend Sally and me as junior air-raid wardens, daylight duty only, meaning that during daytime drills, we could be sent out as messengers. We had armbands and certificates, and we felt very important, although we never did see action.

Our telephone was part of the county's "land telephone communications system." As such, we were a dispatch center for the air-raid signals coming in from the state or county civil defense centers. We never left the phone unattended. Whoever in the house happened to take the first warning call was instructed to get my mother to the phone immediately. She relayed the call to key people in the surrounding communities.

There were four color-coded signals that could come over the phone: the preliminary "yellow" air-raid message, which was the first call to come into our home; the "blue-light" caution, which came 15 minutes later; the "red" message of warning, which meant that an enemy attack was under way; and finally, the "white" all-clear signal. The signals were sounded as 5-second blasts with 3-second intervals over a period of 2 minutes. Sirens or whistles were set up in communities throughout the county, but some rural areas were out of reach of the blasts, and this was a troublesome problem for the civil defense council.

Most of the air-raid exercises were planned, although some were unexpected. Sometimes the state civil defense council determined when they would be conducted, and sometimes the county council initiated a drill. At first, the dates and times were advertised extensively in the local newspapers.

Follow-ups on the drill's successes and problems appeared over the next few days, after the civil defense committee had met to review the situation.

An ongoing problem was the inability to hide the lights of the kilns at the brickworks. Also, some businesses refused to cooperate with the "lights out" order and were fined. And there was an occasional problem with lighted passenger trains crossing the bridge over the Juniata, thus exposing the bridge.

Though the drills were taken seriously, they did have their comic moments—especially drills that caught us by surprise. One summer day in 1943, my aunt, uncle and two cousins were visiting us from Philadelphia. My uncle liked to tease, and my aunt often became impatient with his antics. Their last name was White, and as such, it was a good target for jokes about the air-raid "white" signal.

On this particular day, my aunt happened to answer the phone when the preliminary warning for an air-raid drill came through. My uncle had walked downtown, and my mother was upstairs, away from the phone. "Air-raid warning yellow," came over the phone line.

"All right, Jack, I know it's you," my aunt replied.

"I repeat, air-raid warning yellow," the voice said.

"Cut it out, Jack. I know it's you. What do you want?" My aunt was in no mood for jokes.

"Ma'am, this is air-raid warning yellow!" The voice was insistent.

"I'll hang up this phone!" my aunt exclaimed.

Fortunately, Mother got to the phone just in time, having heard my aunt's side of the conversation. My dad had some explaining to do at the next civil defense meeting, but he straightened things out, and our house continued to be a telephone dispatch center until the war ended.

My friends have memories of their fathers serving in various volunteer civil defense jobs. Besides the air-raid wardens, there were civilian plane spotters, who were trained to look for and identify aircraft flying in the vicinity. Some of my friends were messengers during the drills.

It was a time of intense patriotism, not only for adults, but for us kids too.

Now I know how fortunate we were that the air-raid drills were only practice and that we never had to endure real bombings, like so many of our generation did in other countries. ❖

Right: Page from *A Handbook for Air Raid Wardens*, 1941, courtesy Janice Tate

The Refuge Room

WHAT TO DO IN AN AIR RAID

At the yellow warning, if you are not already on duty, you will be summoned to your post and will carry out orders until relieved. However, here are the rules for those who do not have assigned duties when the air raid warning comes. Memorize them carefully so that you can in turn instruct others. Here is what to tell them:

1. If away from home, seek the nearest shelter. Get off the street.

2. If you are driving, first park your car at the curb; be sure all lights are shut off.

3. If you are at home, send the others to the refuge room. This should be a comfortable place with as little window exposure as possible, equipped with drinking water, things to read, toilet facilities, a flashlight, a portable radio, a sturdy table, and food if you like.

4. Turn off all gas stove burners but leave pilot lights, water heaters and furnaces alone. Leave electricity and water on. Fill some large containers or a bathtub with water.

5. Check up on blackout arrangements. Don't let a crack of light show to the outside.

6. See that everyone's eyeglasses and dentures are in the refuge room. There should be additional warm garments for everyone, too.

7. Keep out of line of windows. Fragments and glass splinters cause most casualties.

8. If bombs fall nearby, get under a heavy table, an overturned davenport.

9. Don't rush out when the "all clear" signal sounds. Maintain the blackout. The Raiders may return.

10. Otherwise, keep cool; be sensible and set an example to others.

Our World at War

By LaVerne Chapman

"Dad is home early," I called to my two sisters, who were busy doing chores in another part of our cozy house. "Hey, something is wrong!" I called out again. "Dad is sick or upset. He didn't unhitch the mule team from the wagon like usual. He didn't even take their harness off so they could eat and drink. He just tied them to the fence!" I hurried to open the door for him.

Sisters Mary and Ann appeared as Dad put the box of supplies on the table. We stood before him, anxiously waiting for him to speak.

Pale and sad-faced, with lips quivering, he said, "Early Sunday morning, the Japanese bombed Pearl Harbor, Hawaii. Many of our people are dead, and more are hurting! The people at the market are afraid they will bomb our West Coast next. Now our world is at war!" He slumped into his chair by the fire and buried his face in his hands. We were not sure if he was crying, or praying, or both.

From the time Dad got the news of the attack on Dec. 7, 1941, our daily routine changed. Now Dad hurried home from town instead of spending most of the day there. In the past, he had lingered to exchange some "man talk" with his cronies at the pool hall and get the latest news and gossip from the local newspaper. He'd have a lunch of cheese with crackers from the cracker barrel at the Kroger grocery store. While he socialized with the owner, the clerks would fill Dad's order and then help carry his purchases to the wagon.

There were also notable changes at the

The author's dad, Monroe Benson, with the family's pig.

one-room school in rural Missouri where we attended classes. Each morning, we pledged allegiance to our flag and to our God, and a prayer was said for our nation. Since that was before television and few families had radios in their homes, our teacher, Miss Mereda, who did have a radio, gave us the latest world news from the night before. We didn't realize then that we were keeping in touch with history as it was being made.

To keep us in touch with the news visually, Miss Mereda hung a giant world map at the front of the classroom. The children in grades one through eight could see it as she used the yardstick to show the nations that were in the news. She pointed to the European nations being overrun by Adolph Hitler's German army, then drew our attention to the islands of the Pacific Ocean, where Japanese suicide attacks killed innocent civilians as well as our servicemen. We listened sadly when our teacher told us that island after island had surrendered to the Japanese.

Dad gradually liquidated our farm equipment and livestock. We moved to Michigan, where the rest of our family lived.

By then, the factories that manufactured everything from clothing to lawn mowers had been transformed into defense plants. I attended school while Dad, Ann and Mary worked as support personnel and served our nation during the remainder of World War II.

Sadly, though, Dad didn't live long enough to see our world at peace again. He died of a massive heart attack on Dec. 9, 1943, two years and two days after our world went to war. ❖

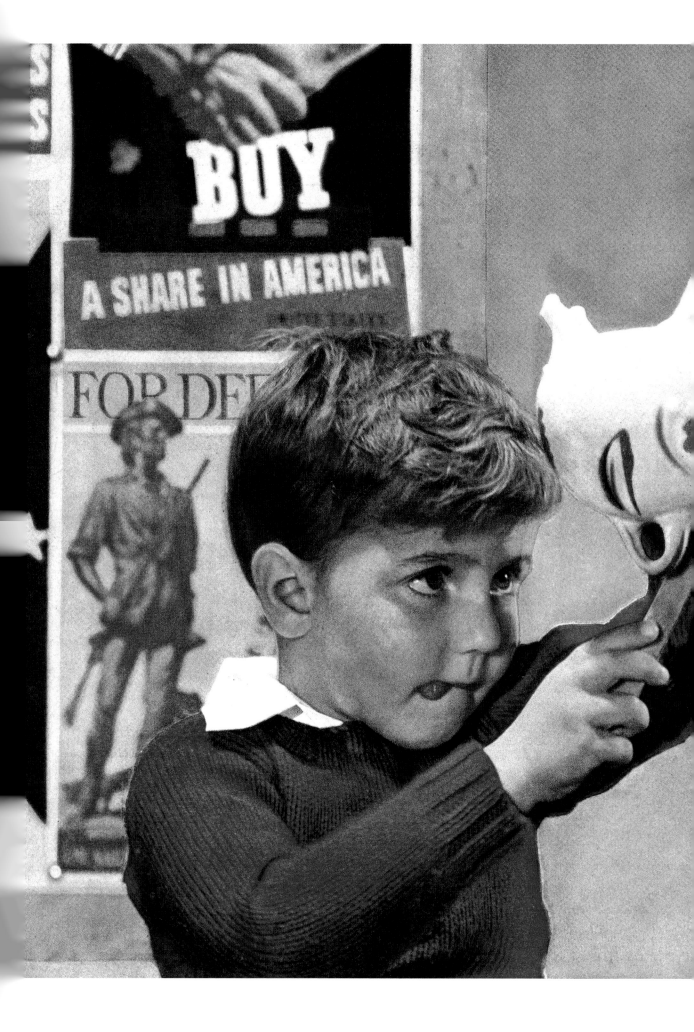

Fighting Families

By Nancy Halstenberg

E very family in America was touched somehow by World War II. Now, from the vantage point of time, it has become its own era, quite significantly, a distinct part of American history. But it wasn't history at the time we lived it; it was our day-to-day existence and reality. Whether serving our country on foreign soil or supporting the war effort from home, we all played a part in it to the best of our abilities.

Like most families, we were around the radio when President Franklin Delano Roosevelt momentously announced the bombing of Pearl Harbor and our entrance into World War II. I can remember, although I was only 9 years old, the drama and impact this radio broadcast had on our lives.

My father led us in prayer. Mama cried, and I had a horrible feeling in the pit of my stomach. Then our lives began to change drastically. We participated in everything we could to help the war effort, including buying stamps and bonds; mine were purchased at school with my allowance and chores money, and Father's at work, the cost deducted from his salary. There were also victory gardens, rationing, saving lard and tinfoil, and writing letters to servicemen.

We watched for the mailman and hoped the news would be good.

I remember these letters so well. We watched for the mailman and hoped the news would be good. And what tears of relief and gladness we shed when a letter arrived and all was well, at least for the time being. We seemed to live from day to day.

My father's brother, Raymond A. Gill, went from the family farm in Albion, Ill., into the Army infantry. He had been a farm boy all his life, and this complete change for him, unfortunately, was only the beginning.

After basic training, he was sent to the European battle zone where, during the invasion of Sicily, he was captured and taken prisoner by the Germans. He had been shot in the leg. He said this saved his life, for most of the men who were taken prisoner from his battalion died along the long march to the prisoner-of-war camps in Germany. Because of his injury, he wasn't able to walk, so he rode in a crowded cattle car on the train from Sicily to Germany. Many men died in the car on the way; the conditions were unbelievably terrible.

Through the Red Cross, we received the news that he was being held in the German POW camp Stalag 1-B. We wrote to him often. Now and then, we would receive solitary postcards from him. We sent many packages to him through the Red Cross. As it turned out, the Germans gave him only a few of our letters and packages. He said they would have all starved if it weren't for the Red Cross. Likewise, we didn't receive all of his messages.

In the prison camp, they taught him how to repair shoes. This was a new occupation for him. He had to work long, arduous hours with little food or rest, but somehow he survived. We prayed for his safety every day, and we wrote letters. When he finally came home at the end of the war, it was a most joyous reunion indeed!

Another occasion that lives forever in my memory is V-J Day, the final end of the atrocious war. Once again, we heard the news on our radio. By this time, I was 13. Father took us to downtown St. Louis, where crowds on the street were yelling, horns were blowing, and paper and confetti were flying everywhere as servicemen of all ranks grabbed girls and kissed them. I've never seen such pandemonium or joy before or since. It was a major experience of my life. I still get carried away when I even think of it.

This war happened during the formative years of my life, important years. To me it brought home the meaning of a united country, a country willing to defend its freedoms. I was very proud to be an American, and I was proud to be part of a family that served its country. ❖

It isn't St. Louis, but the photograph below was captured by Dick DeMarsico in New York City's Times Square on V-J Day, Aug. 14, 1945. Photo courtesy the Library of Congress.

A Time to Remember

By Isabelle Loar Farnham

Looking back, I marvel at the waves of hysteria that engulfed my little Iowa town in 1942. Hitler was transcendent in Europe. England had been under attack, and London lay in ruins. Poland was the site of horrors too grim to be believed. These facts we could learn from the radio and from Pathe newsreels in movie theaters.

The author as newspaper society editor, circa 1941.

But what did that have to do with Iowa Falls, half a world away from such atrocities? A great deal, it seemed, and my community was not the only one to be galvanized into action by the dread of a German invasion.

Invasion? Of course! Everyone firmly believed that the madman of Europe would eventually land ships and submarines on our shores and send his tanks rolling through the small towns and farmlands of eastern and middle America.

The Red Cross held classes to teach everyone first-aid techniques to use after an attack. The handbooks had pictures showing the pressure points we could press to stop bleeding.

We tore up old bed sheets to make slings for broken arms. Nurses gave demonstrations on how to bandage heads, chests, legs. We learned how to improvise stretchers and how to use canes and crutches.

But the most critical training was received at the alarm center. In case of attack, phones would be manned there day and night, and a central command post would be set up to route incoming alarms. I was on duty on at least one occasion, taking and receiving preplanned calls as if our lives depended on them. The windows in the room were covered with blankets so that no stray light would betray our position, and we worked by the light of lamps or flashlights.

We were serious. As editor of the weekly newspaper, I was in on planning the techniques for handling all this information.

I even felt the premonition of impending doom on a personal level. I worried about my mother back in Dewitt, Iowa, and what she would do if armies overran that tiny town and drove the residents on forced marches to prison camps. My mother was old; she had rheumatic knees. I couldn't conceive of her struggling to keep up with other prisoners on such a march, even with soldiers threatening her with guns. Perhaps she would die under the stress. It was a horrible thought.

History has already analyzed Hitler and found him to be a megalomaniac whose rantings and ravings should have been silenced as they were uttered. The realization that it didn't have to be that way is small consolation for those who were caught up in the fearful whirlwind.

Would we be any smarter today if something similar were to happen again? I often wonder. ❖

Neighborhood Bomb Shelter

By Betty Kossick

After the Japanese attack on Pearl Harbor on Dec. 7, 1941, America was forever changed. Its sense of security was fragmented—after all, Hawaii wasn't far from our western shores (although it hadn't yet become our 50th state). I was a 10-year-old child living in Akron, Ohio, when America entered World War II. Akron was known as "The Rubber Capital of the World." The largest rubber factories—Firestone, Goodyear and Goodrich—and the smaller ones as well, were a crucial link in the chain that supplied badly needed equipment to our fighting men and women in the military. Akronites were very patriotic and supportive of the war effort.

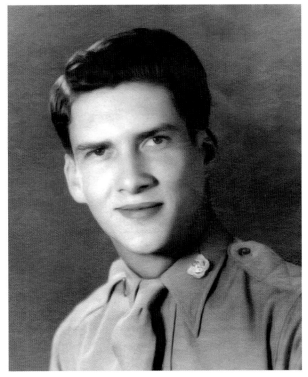

Warrant Officer Leon W. Biss.

My mother was a new factory worker at the Firestone Tire and Rubber Co. In fact, it was the war that provided her with the job that she needed as an unskilled divorced mother. In short time, though, she became a fast and proficient "piece worker."

I remember how she cried the night the news hawkers went to the streets selling the hot-off-the-press accounts of the Pearl Harbor attack. Her tears were for her kid brother, Leon Biss, whom she hadn't seen since he was a little boy. But she knew that he was stationed at Hickam Air Field, and she feared for his life. Fortunately, he came through the attack unharmed.

After Pearl Harbor, Americans feared the possibility of bombs being dropped on the mainland. This was probably of more concern in towns such as Akron, where factories produced so much of what the Armed Forces needed—and the enemy didn't want to have produced. We felt that we might be targeted. Thus bomb shelters were a big topic of conversation.

At school we had air-raid drills on a regular basis. I still can feel the sense of urgency that was instilled in us as our school principal announced the drills. We knew that this was serious; we certainly weren't playing games, although it might have looked like we were playing when we crouched with our knees against our faces and our hands covering our heads.

Our teacher's tone of voice always added to the suspense. We kids didn't know it, but while we were going to school and taking part in these drills, Firestone workers actually were building a bomb shelter. On March 2, 1942, just three months after the United States entered the war, Akron announced that its first bomb shelter had been built near the Firestone factory at Firestone Boulevard and South Main Street—just around the corner from ordinary neighborhoods.

Patterned after the bomb shelters of London, which had survived relentless attacks by German aircraft, the new shelter was hailed as a lifesaving retreat where 50 people could safely wait out an attack. (We didn't yet know what an atom bomb could do—and we *certainly* didn't know what terrorists could do.)

It actually took only a few days to build that shelter. It was constructed of Armco steel using hand tools, and it was shaped like a capsule, 60 feet long and 7½ feet in diameter. It was covered with 3 feet of dirt and settled in a shallow ditch.

Inside, it was equipped with everything from a chemical toilet to board games to give the occupants something to do while they were confined.

Thousands of people toured that bomb shelter, including 15,000 the first week. Some days, as many as 5,000 people came through. My mother went through it, but she wouldn't take me; she said that I might get too frightened. Frightened? She didn't know the half of what we kids made of the scary possibilities of bomb shelters!

Leaflets given to the visitors explained the various features of the bomb shelter's scientific design. In fact, blueprints were given to interested parties. The Firestone Co. received thousands of requests for copies of the shelter's plans. In an article published by the *Akron Beacon Journal* on March 7, 2005, which commemorated the opening of that shelter, staff writer Mark J. Price asked, "Who knows how many were built across the country? Who knows if any are still left?" I'm with him; it would be interesting to know, wouldn't it?

Price reported that the Akron bomb shelter's last known use was as a storage space for vegetables—and he notes that they must have been the best-guarded vegetables in town. Indeed! But thank goodness the scary scenarios we kids came up with never came to pass for Akron's residents. ❖

Firestone Tire and Rubber Co., Akron, Ohio.

That Sunday Afternoon

By Floyd C. Moore

At about 1:30 on the afternoon of Dec. 7, 1941, my wife and I had started out for the Sunday-afternoon movie in the little town of Canton, Okla. I was stationed there with the U.S. Army Corps of Engineers. We were constructing a flood-control dam on the North Canadian River. I was a shift supervisor in charge of construction on the midnight–to–8 a.m. shift.

En route to the theater, we stopped at the town's only drugstore for a Coke. The clerk on duty looked at us, and in a rather disturbed and nervous tone of voice, asked, "Did you know that Japan bombed Pearl Harbor today?"

Surprised and aghast, we answered, "No! We haven't been listening to the radio today."

Canton was a very small town, with only about 600 white people and approximately 300 Native Americans from the Cheyenne and Arapaho tribes living in the area.

Word soon spread, especially among our Corps of Engineers and the contractor's people connected with the construction. There were about 36 persons with the corps and approximately 40 with the contractor.

"Did you know that Japan bombed Pearl Harbor today?"

The corps' construction and administration office was about 2 miles from the heart of the little town. I told my wife we had better drive out there to see if there was any word about the attack at the resident engineer's office.

I found the office open. R.R. Randolph, resident engineer in charge, was there, and he informed me that the district engineer, Col. C.H. Chorpening, had called all the resident engineers that morning from his office in Tulsa and had informed them about the attack after receiving official word from the War Department. His orders were to proceed with their assignments and construction until further official word was received from Washington.

Randolph told me to report for work as usual that night. But he also told me that it was quite possible that our peacetime project might soon be shut down, and that we would be transferred over to military construction.

Well, there was no movie for us that day. We returned to our small upstairs apartment at the home of Lawrence Gray, assistant postmaster of Canton. That night, before I prepared to go to work at 11:30 p.m., Gray's wife and two sons, and my wife sat in their front room, listening to the late news about the attack blaring from the little Atwater Kent radio.

Believe me, everything we heard was bad. It seemed that Japan was ready to invade our West Coast, as "Jap" submarines and aircraft were plying the waterfront along California. This was indeed later verified. History shows that they missed a good chance for an invasion, as we were unprepared. And in Washington, just before the attack, Japanese envoys were conferring with our Secretary of State, Tennessee's Cordell Hull. In fact, they were meeting with him at practically the same time Pearl Harbor was being bombed by the sneak attack.

One of the top radio news announcers at that time was Gabriel Heatter. His favorite opening generally was: "Ah, there's good news tonight." On this day of infamy, however, his program began: "Good evening, folks … there's bad news tonight."

Then there was Walter Winchell, whose trademark greeting was, "Good evening, Mr. and Mrs. America, and all the ships at sea." Also there was the Germanic-toned H.V. Kaltenborn, who never failed to prophesy on things to come. That night in December, they were all giving it as it was, and all the news was shrouded in gloom.

When I reported to work that night, many of the men on the project wanted to volunteer and go whip the "Japs," although war had not yet been officially declared.

As it turned out, we were shut down by the War Production Board soon after war was declared. We Corps of Engineers employees were sent to various areas to build airports and munitions plants.

That was a Sunday afternoon that laid fear in most U.S. citizens' hearts and minds. ❖

The USS Arizona *sinks after the Japanese attack on Pearl Harbor on that "date which will live in infamy," Dec. 7, 1941.*

My Mother's Prayer

By Don C. Miller

I think most of us have fond, lasting memories of our mothers. As a boy growing up in a rural community in East Tennessee, I heard a sacred song entitled *If I Could Hear My Mother Pray Again*. I remember the tune, but very few of the words. I do recall one line, however: "How glad I'd be, it would mean so much to me, if I could hear my mother pray again."

The lot of a housewife and mother in the Depression years of the 1930s was not an easy one. I often wonder how she was able to cope and still face her daily chores with a smile on her face and a song in her heart. Often I heard her singing *When You and I Were Young, Maggie*, Gene Autry's *Mexicali Rose* or *Kneel at the Cross*. Now I know her ability to handle life in such a positive way was the result of her steadfast faith in God.

Each night before retiring, she knelt at her bedside and said a prayer to the Almighty. Before asking for any further blessings, she always thanked God for blessings already received. Then she proceeded to ask for forgiveness and for the Lord to watch over, bless and protect us.

My father had died in August 1939. The following August, in 1940, my older brother, Phillip, enlisted in the Army. With Phillip in the Army and our country involved in World War II shortly thereafter, Mother's nightly prayer took on another dimension. In addition to her regular prayer, she said a special prayer for her son and for all the young people in the military who were willing to lay their lives on the line for the cause of freedom.

Phillip was a paratrooper. He jumped onto French soil in the early hours of D-Day in 1944. Unable to find the main body of their regiment, he and several others in his outfit were captured by the Germans.

Not long after D-Day, Mother received word that her son was missing in action. It was several weeks later before we learned that Phillip was a prisoner of war. In the meantime, we were not sure if my brother was dead or alive. But my mother's faith was undeterred.

Germany surrendered on May 8, 1945, and Phillip came home early that June. His return was proof to my mother that her faith and prayers had not been in vain.

My mother died at age 90 in April 1991. I have many pleasant memories of her, but the most beautiful and vivid is that of my mother's nightly bedside prayer. ❖

In this family photo taken in the summer of 1936, the author's mother is second from the left in the back row. The author's dad is seated, and his brother Phillip is in the front on the far right. He is crying because he didn't want to be in the photo.

The Day the Germans Came

By Don Haines

It was a sunny summer day when they brought the German soldiers to our farm. They came in two open trucks, with American soldiers as their guards. They were called POWs (prisoners of war), and they had come to pick our string beans. The year was 1944, and I was 9.

I knew the Germans were coming. I'd listened intently while my father talked about it, and then I'd lain awake much of the night, wondering what they'd look like.

For two and a half years I'd been hearing about the Germans and the Japs, how they'd started the war because they wanted to take over the world.

Hitler was the leader of the Germans, and Tojo was the leader of the Japs. They had to be defeated; otherwise they'd take over our country, and things would never be the same. Things like that can be scary for a kid of 9. When you're 9, you don't want things to *ever* change.

I'd watched as most of the adult males in my life went away to war. When I asked when they were coming home, nobody knew. "When the war is over," was the standard answer.

I tried to do my part. I put less sugar on my oatmeal—it was rationed. I saved rubber and aluminum. I went door-to-door, asking for old newspapers and magazines. I bought war stamps and pasted them in a book ("Lick a stamp—slap a Jap"). I read an issue of *Life* magazine that told of German spies being captured in New Jersey, and I wondered what these Germans had against us. My hatred was growing daily. That's why, when I heard they were coming to our farm, I knew I had to see them.

I didn't ask permission from my parents like 9-year-olds are supposed to do. I guess I thought it was my war, too, and I had a right to see these people who had brought so much darkness to my bright little world. I didn't have a plan. I didn't want to talk to them. I just had to *see* them!

The author at age 10 in 1945.

As I approached the bean field, I noticed my father standing at the far end, talking to an American soldier who was holding a rifle. I knew the men bending over the bean rows had to be the Germans. They were talking to one another, but I couldn't understand what they were saying.

Then I heard the words *"der kinder."* With that, one of the Germans stood up, took off his cap, turned toward me and gave a smile that has stayed with me for 55 years.

"Guten tag," he said, still smiling. I didn't speak, but raised my hand in greeting. That was the extent of our interaction.

I left the bean field still hating Germans—except one. It's hard to hate a man who smiles at you. When I got back to the house, my mother asked where I'd been. "I went to see the Germans," I replied.

"What did they look like?"

I thought of the smile and the words I didn't understand. "They look like us." ❖

For the Boys

Chapter Two

The war brought out the best in people as everyone pulled together for our brave troops fighting in remote parts of the world. Some attempts to do things "for the boys" turned romantic and others turned amusing, like this story by Muriel Calegari published in *Good Old Days* magazine in 1997. She gave a young naval officer "Something to Remember Me By":

"During World War II, I served as a hostess at an officers' club in Washington, D.C. We were required to dance at least once with any officer who asked us.

"Many of the men were good dancers, some exceptionally good. Richard Greenby was a very good dancer. A firm and smooth leader, he had me twirling, swinging and gliding with a rhythm I didn't know I possessed. He sought me out frequently, and I was a willing partner.

"After a few weeks, Richard asked, 'Are you allowed to date officers you meet here?'

"I replied, 'We are not permitted to leave the club with an officer, but are allowed to use our discretion about fraternizing on our own time.'

"This produced an invitation for dinner and dancing at the Shoreham Hotel the following Saturday. Glenn Miller and his orchestra were there that night. I was ecstatic!

"While dressing, I sprang a run in my last pair of nylons. What was I going to do?

"Suddenly, my puddling eyes fell on my roommate's bottle of leg makeup. She had urged me to try it. It was liquid, in a coffee brown shade. I applied it from my toes to about 6

After a few weeks, Richard asked, "Are you allowed to date officers you meet here?"

inches above my knees. In front of the mirror, I admired my new, run-proof leg coverings.

"Richard looked splendid in his dress whites. Our dinner conversation was stimulating with exchanged questions about backgrounds, interests and vague future plans. Richard said he was being shipped out in three weeks and lamented we had so little time.

"Glenn Miller played the popular tunes of the day, and we danced almost every dance. Too soon, *Goodnight Sweetheart* signaled the end of the dancing.

"While the taxi waited, Richard kissed me goodnight at the door and said he would call soon. As he turned away, I noticed several coffee-colored smudges on his white pants. I quickly closed the door.

"Moving to the window, I watched him standing under the streetlight looking down at his pants. He pulled forward the left inseam and the right. He hit his forehead with the heel of his hand, shook his head back and forth, and hurled himself into the idling cab.

"The next day, my roommate told me I should have patted my legs with a towel after applying the makeup.

"Somehow I knew I wouldn't hear from Richard again—and I didn't. After three weeks I gave up. Disappointed, I thought, *Why couldn't he have been an Army man? Coffee brown smudges wouldn't show on an Army uniform*."

From USO clubs to celebrity shows, the memories in this chapter reflect the great honor it was just to do anything we could "For the Boys."

—*Ken Tate*

The Hollywood Canteen

By Joseph Curreri

When you think of Hollywood in wartime, you think of Bob Hope, Abbott and Costello, Carole Lombard, Captain Clark Gable, Lieutenant Commander Robert Montgomery and Brigadier General Jimmy Stewart. Some of the biggest stars went off to fight, and others stayed home to entertain and build morale.

But in between was the Hollywood Canteen, which provided pure entertainment for troops on temporary leave from the fighting.

"The night we opened, hundreds of servicemen came, and we knew that we had a going thing," said Bette Davis, who, along with John Garfield, founded the Hollywood Canteen. From opening day, it was the most popular show in town. Most every star in Hollywood showed up for duty at the Canteen—to do dishes, cook, serve troops, scrub floors and entertain.

The Canteen offered servicemen and women on furlough a real nightclub where major movie actors rolled up their sleeves and pitched in for the sake of the deserving soldier or sailor. "I was thrilled for them," said Bette Davis. "All the people gave so much of their time to entertain, make them laugh and forget. All the stars were very aware, very concerned."

> *Some of the biggest stars went off to fight, and others stayed home to entertain and build morale.*

I was a 22-year-old wide-eyed airman back then, and I'll never forget. Stationed at nearby Santa Monica, I went to the Canteen every chance I got. I saw what I wanted to see—movie stars! I wrote in my dusty diary: *What a thrill to stand up close to them, talk with them, laugh with them. They were so real: Gary Cooper, so modest and shy; Basil Rathbone, so debonair; beautiful June Lang (she kissed me!); Marlene Dietrich, who danced with me, and when I was cut in by other soldiers, I cut right back. "You again!" she laughed.*

Who would believe it, back home or in my outfit, when I bragged, "I held Marlene Dietrich and June Lang in my arms"?

The day Basil Rathbone was there, he signed autographs by the hour and was perspiring. When I went to him for an autograph, I commented, "Don't you wish you had a shorter name?" He laughed and said, "Yes, like an *X*." Another time, John Garfield told us he'd just finished working on love scenes with Ann Sheridan. He said with a grin, "I had a hard day, a hard day."

There were Charlie McCarthy and Edgar Bergen, Patricia Morrison, Burns and Allen, Ginny Simms, Marsha Hunt and Eddie Cantor, just to name a few. Most remembered was Red Skelton, doing his drink-tasting routine. "Ladies and gentlemen," he began, pretending to be a radio pitchman, "this is the *Guzzler's Gin Program*. Try Guzzler's Gin, the college drink—one bottle and you're in a class by yourself! Try it." He did … and almost choked. With each commercial for Guzzler's Gin, he grew more plastered, spraying himself and the stage (including myself) with his product, staggering cross-eyed and babbling nonsense.

Other unforgettable performances were the Andrews Sisters singing *Boogie Woogie Bugle Boy of Company B,* and the famous baseball routine of Abbot and Costello's *Who's on First?*

It was unreal. Here I was, a skinny kid from South Philadelphia, and I was greeted at the door by Lana Turner, Deanna Durbin and Dinah Shore. Every Saturday they'd have a bingo game—and the M.C. was cackling Kay Kyser. Linda Darnell served servicemen dinner and said "Hello" and smiled at me.

Servicemen could have a hamburger with John Garfield or dance to the music of famous orchestras like those of Rudy Vallee, Tommy Dorsey or Xavier Cugat. When Edgar Bergen and Charlie McCarthy broke in for a sudden appearance, Charlie's eyes popped out as he ogled the beautiful starlets as much as the servicemen did.

George Raft washed dishes. Even Vice President Henry Wallace once joined the second shift in the kitchen.

The popularity of the club even inspired movies, appropriately titled *Hollywood Canteen* and *Stage Door Canteen*.

The Department of Defense later decorated Bette Davis with the Public Service Medal and announced that more than a million servicemen and women were entertained by movie-colony figures each year. They entertained us, brought us a touch of home, built our morale and left us with lifelong memories. ❖

USO camp shows drew a full house wherever they played. Courtesy United Service Organizations Inc.

Accentuate the Positive

By Marie Cole Colasuonno

After completing a tour of duty with the United States Navy in the South Pacific, my husband was stationed at Sun Valley, Idaho, toward the end of World War II. At that time, it was common practice for celebrities to entertain the troops, and we happened to be in the right place at the right time. Little did I know that I—with a love of music, but no formal training—was about to enter my own combat zone! I wrote a letter dated June 26, 1945, to my family describing the event:

Dear Family,

Well, you'd better hang on to your hats, because I really have a yarn to spin! Last Sunday noon George and I went out to the Lodge as usual for dinner, and just as we walked in the lobby, there stood the captain. He came toward us solemnly and said, "Have you had the word?" Thinking something calamitous had happened, we said "no" in some anxiety.

"Bing Crosby is coming here this afternoon at 2:15," he said.

I was thrilled (who wouldn't be?) and said, "How wonderful!"

"And," the captain went on, fixing me with an eagle eye, "he wants an accompanist. Could you help out?"

> *Before I knew what was happening, he gave me a big smack, right there in front of everybody.*

Well, you could have heard my stomach drop to my boots. I began spluttering and expostulating, and then I realized George was looking at me peculiarly and the captain was getting frosty around the edges. So I began to try to switch needles in midstream or something, and get around to "Why, of course, I'd be glad to do whatever I could," all the time swallowing egg-sized lumps in my throat.

The captain went on to explain that he had asked two other people to meet with our celebrity so he could take his pick. The other two warned me in advance that if he didn't have any music, I was it!

Well, we went up to eat a beautiful steak and strawberries, but as far as I was concerned, they were just straw. I could probably pick out most pieces he wanted, but in the keys I was used to—and if he wanted them different … .

Well, finally 2:15 arrived, and so did Mr. Crosby, flanked by the two captains, the other two people and one frightened guppy—me.

The captain said, "Mr. Crosby, this is Woods, Jones and Mrs. Colasuonno. Miss Woods plays by music, Jones can play sacred music and

Mrs. C. can play with music or without."

So we began to talk it over, and Bing said, "How about *Too-Ra-Loo-Ra-Loo-Ra* in the key of A?"

I said, "Well, I don't know anything about the keys. What note does it start on?"

He said, "Gosh, I don't know. We're a fine pair of musical illiterates, aren't we?"

I said, "Well, if you can tell me the note it starts on, I could make out, I guess." So we went into where the piano was and he made a list, and I said, "Write down C."

Top: Bing's autograph was written just below the list of songs. Below: Taking a bow with Bing at Sun Valley in 1945.

To Marie
The Greatest
accompanist in
Sun Valley
Bing Crosby

So he grinned and wrote down C. We had the music, but it was all about two notes too high. And all the keys he wanted to sing in were unfamiliar to me—I could just barely hit a note here and a note there. But he patted me on the shoulder encouragingly and said, "That's fine, fine. You're doing great."

I was sitting there sweating blood, with the other two stubbornly insisting they couldn't do it. Well, I want to say that Mr. Crosby is a gentleman. For sheer unadulterated courtesy to a scared green nobody, he takes the cake.

Well, we ran through the list—no practicing, nothing—and about 15 minutes after he arrived, we were lined up inside the lodge, waiting to go out to the open-air pavilion after the captain introduced him.

I managed to stagger out behind Bing and fall into a chair in front of the piano, and put my list up in front of me while he was telling how he just left "The Guy with the Nose" (Bob Hope) down in Salt Lake.

He rambled on for a few jokes about his racehorses. He said he had just bought one when all of a sudden, it collapsed as he was leading it away. He said he had to stick around, even if it was dying, to finally be able to see the finish of one of his horses!

Then he turned to me and said, "How about *Accentuate the Positive*?" Fortunately I managed to chord that one pretty well. The rest of the program was a daze, except that he made me stand up and take a bow with him somewhere.

At the end of Bing's speech, the captain went into a speech about how "Mrs. Colasuonno graciously helped out."

Then Mr. Crosby pulled me up alongside him and the captain, and before I knew what was happening, he gave me a big smack, right there in front of everybody! Well, that really finished me off! So now when my husband brags about how he danced with Betty Grable once, I can blithely reply, "That's nothing! Bing Crosby kissed me!"

Well, actually I really murdered the whole thing, but as I say, he was grand about it all, the soul of courtesy, as all those big shots seem to be, and even wrote me a little inscription on the list of songs: "To Marie, the greatest accompanist in Sun Valley, Bing Crosby."

Since there are probably all of 500 people in the Valley, that isn't saying much, but it's fun to have, and will be something to tell my grandchildren. Actually I think it all took 10 years off my life.

Much love,
Marie ❖

A Brush With Greatness

By Mary Ostopak

My cousin, Steve (right), had just started in the Army for basic training. He made many friends, and they decided to take some pictures one day, horsing around, as usual.

Some guy came over to them.
"May I get in your picture?" he asked.
"Sure," they answered.

It wasn't until the picture was developed later that they realized "the guy" was the one and only Der Bingle, Bing Crosby (middle).

They then remembered that Bing had been on the base that day to do a show for them. ❖

Angels at the Water Tower

By Francis X. Sculley

"Compan-*eee*, 'ten-*hutt*!" barked the first sergeant. Then, over the loudspeaker, came the resonant voice of the commandant of the Topeka Air Base. "May I take this opportunity to wish each of you men a very merry Christmas and the most successful of all New Years. Let us all pray to Almighty God that the job underway will be brought to a successful conclusion, so that by next Christmas, we will all be home with our loved ones again. To those of you on the detachment that is shipping tonight, my very special wishes. Goodbye, and God bless you."

"A lot *he* cares, up there in the officers' club, sipping on hot Tom-and-Jerries, with some blonde on his knee, and we're shipping on Christmas Eve," muttered a voice from the rear ranks that could be heard a block away. "They don't even give us a name; we're just 'casuals'! Bull feathers!"

"You're still at attention, men!" admonished the sergeant in a voice that sounded almost human. "At ease, while the chaplain leads us in prayer."

The detachment stood silent in the snow as the padre led us in prayer. Down in the railroad yard, a long string of cars was switched onto a siding as a switchman waved his lantern. Once or twice, a muffled sob could be heard from the ranks of the kids, many of whom were spending their first Christmas away from home.

"Merry Christmas, boys!" waved one of the ladies, as she struggled with the coffeemaker.

"All right, men, pick up your gear and move out at route step. Let's show these rear-echelon commandos that we're real soldiers. Everybody sing!" exhorted Sgt. Harry Fain. He was tougher than a 60-cent steak, but one of the most efficient non-coms this writer ever met.

"*Sing*, I said!" roared Fain, reverting to type.

"Around the corner, she pushed a baby carriage; she pushed it in the springtime and in the month of May; she pushed it for her soldier, who was far, far away, far away, far away," we refrained.

And so the troops moved to the railroad siding. Once more we had roll call while the men danced up and down in the snow and bitter cold.

"Imagine making those cows sleep in the field on a cold night like this, while we take their nice warm car. Hey, getta load of those cars!

Jesse James must've boarded one of those, and we gotta ride all the way to New York in 'em!" wailed the detachment's ace griper.

"Men, there isn't enough bunk space for all of us. Some of you will have to sit up all night, and then tomorrow you can switch. Sorry, but that's the way it is," lamely explained a transportation corps non-com, who walked up and down the line of boarding troops.

"Shipping on Christmas Eve! Of all the harebrained things this man's Army ever did!" groused our No. 1 griper.

"Hey, 4-F, Washington crossed the Delaware on Christmas night," came a voice from the rear.

"Yeah, he did. But there were no U-boats in the Delaware!" shouted back our boy.

Soon we boarded the train and headed through the port of embarkation and the waiting transports. So the train groped its way across the state of Kansas. With all the window shades down, we couldn't see the signs of activity outside; although, once in a while, we could hear a few voices from the station platforms as they wished each other a merry Christmas.

Some of the boys had already hit the sack, while the rest of us tried to make ourselves comfortable in the straight-back chairs of the century-old day-coach.

A cold draft swept down the aisle, making sleep almost impossible, and we all huddled a little closer to keep warm. Few wanted to go through the agony of breaking up the horseshoe pack to get their blankets, so we just threw our topcoats over one another.

It was 3 o'clock on my Ingersol when the train came to a grinding halt, almost throwing some of us out of the chairs. Suddenly, the door between our coach and the adjoining car opened and a lanky Southern youth stuck in his head.

"We're stoppin' for water. There's a whole bunch of ladies out there in the snow with candy and cigarettes, hot coffee, sandwiches and a whole bunch of things. Everybody out!" he bellowed, and then he slammed the door.

I snatched my overcoat from the back of a sleeping buddy and headed for the end of the car and out to the steps leading from the coach.

"Maybe some of 'em have boys in the service, just like us ..."

Outside, in knee-deep snow, there were at least two dozen women, most of whom looked old enough to be grandmothers. As far as the eye could see, there wasn't a sign of habitation anywhere. Down the tracks there was a big water tower; and "Old Faithful," as we had named the iron steed, was taking on water.

"Do you like fruitcake, soldier boy? Here's a bag of candy, some cigarettes, and if you step over in the line, you can have a nice, hot cup of coffee and a sandwich," said a gray-haired lady in a voice that seemed to be straight from heaven.

As some of us shuffled uneasily at all of the feminine attention, we saw dozens of cardboard boxes, loaded with tissue-wrapped packages.

"It must've taken them days to wrap those things, and who put up the money for it? Look, they dragged them through the snow-covered field to this tower. Imagine that! Some of 'em have families at home, and they're out here with an outfit that doesn't even have a name. You just can't beat American people," was the soft comment of the company complainer.

"Maybe some of 'em have boys in the service, just like us, only they don't know where they are tonight. Well, here's hopin' someone is lookin' out for 'em like they have for us," said our ex-bartender.

Suddenly, the train whistle sounded and the bell started to clang.

"All aboard, men!" shouted Fain, as he pegged away on a cigar given to him by one of the ladies.

"Merry Christmas, boys!" waved one of the ladies, as she struggled with the coffeemaker. "We have another train to meet tomorrow night, so we'll have to get back to town. God bless all of you!"

"We'll never forget you, ladies! We can't send you a card, as we don't know who you are, or where you live," shouted one of the troops from the coach platform before the door banged shut. "We'll never forget the Angels at the Water Tower!"

And we never did. ❖

"Keep Me Safe Tonight"

By Ruth Cox Anderson

During World War II, I was going to a small Lutheran college. The only men were disabled or were seminarians. No seminarian was interested in dating a Methodist girl, so I went to the YMCA dances.

I started out each evening praying: "Dear God, Blessed Virgin Mary, and all the good fairies that look after wild little Irish girls, keep me safe tonight." Methodists didn't pray to Mary, but I liked the sound of the phrase "wild little Irish girl." Mama, who had died when I was 11, had been Irish.

One evening at the Y, a sailor asked me to dance. We were engaged in an animated discussion of Lord Byron's poetry, so I danced with him a second time—and then a third. Realizing I had broken my usual pattern of dancing only once with a partner, I pleaded fatigue and asked to be excused. With boyish gallantry and manly insistence, he said that he would see me home.

He was good-looking, courteous, polite, obviously from a good family. He was quite insistent, and I was flattered. After all, it was early enough that the streetcar probably would be more than half-full. When I said he might see me home, his face lit up with delight.

As we left the safety of the Y, my mind began to light up with stories I had heard about sailor boys. The streetcar seat wasn't any wider than necessary to hold two bodies, but there were people around. The lights were bright, and my sailor was telling me how glad he was to have met such a nice girl. He intended to write all about it to his mother on Sunday afternoon.

When we came to the campus stop, I turned in the streetcar door and said, "Thank you for riding out here with me. It's only a few steps to the dorm." But he eased quickly past me and down the step, then held out his hand and helped me down.

"I'll see you to your door," he said. After a short walk, he gave my arm a sudden tug and I was seated beside him on a campus bench. His arm went around me.

"Let's not sit here," I said. "I want to get home."

"Why are you so nervous?" he asked, snuggling me closer. At that moment, it occurred to me that God, Mary and all the fairies might be busy in other places. That was when I looked up and saw the gray-haired little lady across the street from campus, sitting in her armchair, knitting.

"This," I said, "is a strict Lutheran school. See that lady in the window across the street?"

"I see her," he said. "So what? She's just sitting there knitting."

"She is chaperone of this bench."

"A likely story," he said smoothly, and clutched me to him. At least he started to. The little lady dropped her knitting, stood up, peered out the window and then started walking away.

"She saw you putting your arm around me," I said. "She is going to phone the security guard. We had better go."

"What kind of school did you say this is?" he asked, standing up.

"Lutheran," I said. "They are very careful of us. Seminarians are trained here, and the school is anxious to see that everyone behaves properly."

We were walking away from our bench when the darling gray-haired lady peered out her window again.

"Let's walk faster," the sailor said.

To this day, I have never been kissed good night by a sailor. It doesn't seem likely that God or the Blessed Virgin would have prompted me to tell a lie. Do you think there really are fairies? ❖

Childhood Memories

By Marilyn J. Smith

*I*n 1941, I was 5 years old, and at such a young and tender age, I didn't have much knowledge about the war that was raging in Europe, or even the horrific events of Pearl Harbor that had brought America into World War II on Dec. 7, 1941.

But war touches everyone, and during the next few years, unforgettable experiences would come into my own little world and remain with me as vivid memories to this day.

The Depression was winding down in 1941, and my parents decided they could afford to give my sister and me music lessons. A man came to our house with sample instruments, and when I saw the small violin, I knew that that was what I wanted to play.

We became band members at the Reitler Music Studio on Colfax Avenue in Denver. My sister chose accordion and was in an all-accordion band. I was five years younger than she was, so I was placed in a different band with all sorts of instruments.

The author in front of her home, wearing her "formal."

I was the youngest member of the band, and I loved it! We did a lot of performing at schools and churches and other functions. My mother made me a beautiful, lilac-colored, floor-length dress, which I called my formal, and because I was so small, they would stand me on a chair in front of the microphone to do my solos, during which I would play the fiddle and sing.

In 1942 or 1943, we were asked to play for wounded servicemen in a big concert at Fitzsimmons Army Hospital. (Some may remember this as the hospital where President Eisenhower recovered from a heart attack years later.)

I remember so well the stage fright I felt when I looked out into that sea of faces from backstage. I thought there must have been thousands of people in the audience.

When our turn finally came, our band played, and I performed my little solo on the chair, *Coming In on a Wing and a Prayer*, which was a very popular song in those days. After our performance, we were allowed to go into the audience and sit with our parents for the rest of the show.

An airman who was sitting next to my parents was very touched by my performance. With tears in his eyes, he told me that I reminded him of his little girl back home. He took his wings pin off his jacket and gave it to me. I knew this was a very special thing for him to do and a big honor for me, so I have always kept the pin.

Our little band was a big hit at the show. Some of us were invited to come back to the hospital and perform for the men who were too ill to attend the concert. We were to go to several wards and walk right in among the patients and entertain them. I was very excited and happy at the prospect, but I was ill-prepared for what I was about to see.

I can never forget walking into that first ward and seeing many men in beds, bandaged from head to toe. One had an arm and leg suspended by wires from a framework around the bed. Others were in wheelchairs and were missing limbs or had suffered disfiguring facial injuries. Many were hooked up to big machines.

From left to right: the author; her mother, Ruby; her father, Wes; and her sister, Lois.

I'm ashamed to say that I was very frightened and upset by all this, and I began to cry. They had to take me out, so I was not able to help cheer these poor men. Whenever I hear anything about war, this is the picture that is indelibly imprinted on my mind, even though that was more than 60 years ago.

Then, not long after that, my dad was drafted! He chose the Navy, and he went to boot camp in San Diego. He was assigned to sea duty on the U.S.S. Yorktown, "The Fighting Lady," as it was called. He remained in the Pacific until the war with Japan was over. We had never been separated before, and his absence was very hard on us. Mother had to go to work, and sometimes she held down two jobs.

We all missed Dad so much, and we worried about him a lot, even though he wrote often and never said anything to worry us. His letters were always cheerful as he told about funny things that happened on the ship, or places he would visit on liberty. Once he drew a picture of a pod of whales he had seen, some of them spouting. He also told of seeing a huge armada of ships as far as the eye could see.

Some of his letters were censored—that is, little holes were cut in them. Some were called "V-mail" and were photocopied on special paper and reduced in size. I recall the little flag we proudly displayed in our front window to show that a U.S. serviceman lived in our house.

I loved the Navy, and I always tried to wear my white sailor dress or my little Wave uniform whenever I could. I sang *Anchors Aweigh* and *Bell-Bottom Trousers* and knew every verse by heart. I remember the words so well:

> Bell-bottom trousers,
> Coat of navy blue,
> I love a sailor,
> And he loves me too.

When the war was over, my mother and I went to San Francisco to meet Dad. My uncle lived there, and so we stayed for several weeks.

I can never forget the many, many, many sailors I saw there, everywhere we went! We got to go aboard ship and take a tour. That ship was gigantic! The room where my Dad worked was dark and filled with radar screens that lit up and blipped—very impressive!

I was 9 years old when the war ended, but my "childhood war memories" have filled me with patriotism and awareness for my whole life. ❖

A Picture's Worth ...

By Carl Baumann

*M*y father was a freelance commercial artist, with a studio in New York City near the ad agencies that commissioned his work. In the early 1940s, the commercial art market demanded increasingly realistic painting, just as color photography was coming into use. As my father's evolving pictorial skills approached photo-realism, his work began to be replaced by color photographs!

Above: The author's father, Ernest Baumann, is pictured at right with other USO artists sketching wounded veterans at Halloran Hospital on Staten Island, N.Y. Facing page: Three examples of typical charcoal portraits from his father's USO days, 1943–1946.

And so it went. Painterly skills would become marketable again about 30 years later, but too late for my father, who by then had ascended (in earthly near-poverty) to that studio of the very finest of arts in heaven.

During World War II, he did several government-commissioned posters for military aircraft plants. Once, when I was home on leave from Navy flight training, he borrowed my aviator's helmet and goggles to dress up a male model as a fighter pilot. Looking skyward, the pilot said to the aircraft workers, "Build more P-38s!"

But my father's commissions were coming farther and farther apart, and the expense of keeping his New York City studio became troublesome.

Wondering what to do about his diminishing income and increasing "spare time," he found that the USO was recruiting artists skilled in portraiture to visit military hospitals as morale boosters, and do pencil or charcoal portraits of recuperating servicemen. The USO would provide room and board, and a modest per diem.

P.F.C. John B Smith.
U-S-O-Camp Shows
-B 3.7.45-

-Pfc. Steven G. Sper.
U.S.O Camp Shows
Baumann.

T.S. Donald Lloyd
Halloran.
Baumann.
11.12.44.

To my father, who was truly expert in portraiture, this was an appealing opportunity. But there was one big catch: The artists, in groups of a dozen or so, would be flown around in military transport planes—and my father suffered from a genuine fear of flying. It was quite common among those born before the airplane.

But with me in flight training at the time, still quite alive and proselytizing about the joys and safety of flight, he fought his fears and soon signed on for the project.

After several visits to veterans' hospitals in the Northeast, he was sent to the Navy hospital at Memphis, Tenn., when I was in primary flight training there. We had a great visit. It was almost like being home on leave. His artists' troupe would be at the Memphis Hospital for a week, and each artist would do six to 12 portraits per day, according to his speed and skill. I accompanied my father to watch him work, and it was a pleasure to behold.

Many of the young patients had never known an "artist," much less seen one at work. They were fascinated by how quickly Dad could conjure up a good likeness of his subjects, some of whom were bedridden, propped up for the occasion.

A crowd of observers appeared, some in wheelchairs or on crutches, and Dad enjoyed talking and joking with them while he worked. It was a good show, clearly a morale booster, as was the USO's intention.

When completed, each portrait was carefully packed and mailed to the subject's person of choice—usually to his mom, wife or sweetheart. Heartfelt appreciation for his work was made amply clear to my father, more so than ever before from his usual commercial clients.

My father later confided that those USO hospital tours were among the happiest days of his life. They were among the happiest days of my life too. ❖

A typical poster from World War II by the author's father, Ernest Baumann.

The following is a typical letter of appreciation received by my father:

April 29, 1946

Dear Mr. Baumann,

This is a brief note of thanks from a grateful mother for your very thoughtful gift. Your wonderful drawing of my son, Cpl. Jesse Dipley, arrived a short time ago. You will never know how thrilled and happy I was when I first saw it. The likeness is remarkable. You may rest assured that your drawing of my boy will be well taken care of, and will be viewed by many.

God bless you for your wonderful work.

Gratefully yours,

Mrs. Mae Dipley

U.S. ARMY
OFFICIAL POSTER

UP AND AT 'EM!

BUILD MORE P-38's

Hollywood's Finest Hour

By Joseph Curreri

*J*ust as we will always remember Sept. 11 and honor the dead from that horrendous attack on the World Trade Center, we can never forget another attack America endured—the date of infamy—and World War II. On Dec. 7, 1941, a Japanese sneak attack turned the "sleeping American giant" into a determined nation of heroes. All the world became a stage. America was united as it had never been before.

And for Hollywood, it was its finest hour. The West Coast was blacked out, even with some false alerts (though everyone didn't take them seriously). "Meatless Tuesday" … "V-mail" … "victory gardens" … "ration stamps"—these strange new terms quickly became part of our vocabulary. We were at war. The men we loved best were going off to serve their country.

America's war machine was fueled by neighborhood scrap and paper drives. "JUNK MAKES FIGHTING WEAPONS" read one poster, and homefront patriots delved into garages, attics and kitchen cupboards to donate old pots and pans, tires, lawn mowers, radiators and even the bumpers off their cars.

Jimmy Stewart (left), the first actor to volunteer in World War II, swears his allegiance. He led 14 raids over enemy territory, rising through the ranks to become a general.

While servicemen gave their lives on the battlefields, Americans at home gave their time and energy. They rolled 2.5 billion bandages, danced with soldiers at USO canteens, took them into their homes for Sunday dinners and visited them in hospitals. They manned rationing boards and draft boards, patrolled their neighborhoods during blackouts, and kept tedious watch for enemy planes that never came. They gave their blood to the Red Cross. Food was rationed. Americans who'd learned just how far they could stretch a meal during the Depression learned to stand in line for meat, coffee, butter and sugar.

If the absence of air raids let Americans sleep in peace, it also gave them time to lie awake and worry about husbands, brothers and sons hunkered down in trenches or huddled in the bellies of planes and ships thousands of miles from home. It also left America free to do what it did best—produce.

The ghosts of Depression-era unemployment were finally laid to rest as 3.5 million women picked up wrenches and acetylene torches, and took their places on the nation's assembly lines.

President Roosevelt estimated the war program for 1942 at "$56 billion—that means taxes and bonds. And bonds and taxes."

Hollywood's influence on the American public was at its peak. War can be hell. Or war can be swell. It all depends on which movie you see.

Academy Award winner Frank Capra marched out of the studios and enlisted in the U.S. Army. As Major Capra, he produced a series of World War II documentaries that would win the highest award the Army can bestow on a noncombatant—the Distinguished Service Medal. His *Why We Fight* orientation films showed why America was in the war, and they proved invaluable in the training of young recruits.

Among others to fall in line was John Huston. As Captain Huston, he filmed *The Battle of San Piedro*, revealing the courage and desperation of the foot soldier. It was an uncompromising look at the face of war. John Ford produced the riveting *Battle of Midway* in 1942, a tribute to America's first sea victory of the war.

Hollywood ground out movies and shorts to "rally 'round the flag," showing motion pictures' power to persuade. Patriotic and morale-building films abounded, such as Irvin Berlin's *This Is the Army*. Songwriter Sammy Cahn wrote the score for *Follow the Boys* and was personally requested by Frank Sinatra to write the score with Jule Styne for *Anchors Aweigh*.

And who could forget the film about George M. Cohan, *Yankee Doodle Dandy*, with James

Bob Hope was the soldier's ultimate entertainer. He frequently entertained at the canteen whenever he wasn't at far-off fronts like this one in Africa.

Cagney? Or the Andrews Sisters' *Boogie Woo-gie Bugle Boy of Company B; You're In the Army, Mr. Jones*; and the biggest of them all, Irving Berlin's *White Christmas*, sung by Bing Crosby in the movie *Holiday Inn*?

To keep fightin' men dreaming of coming home for Christmas, photos of wives, sisters, sweethearts and mothers adorned every foot-locker, barracks shelf and wall. Hollywood star-lets shared that adoration. Rita Hayworth pro-jected the steamy image of "the love goddess," and Betty Grable was No. 1 on walls *and* the big screen as "America's pinup girl."

While soldiers drooled, Bob Hope and others kept them laughing with USO tours in every cor-ner of the globe. By the end of the war, perform-ers had given more than 300,000 shows—all to relieve the tension and loneliness of battle—even risking their lives touring remote areas and battlefields to entertain war-weary troops.

Yes, Hollywood did its share. Studios played an invaluable part in the war effort. While some of their biggest stars went off to fight, others stayed home to entertain and to build morale, a weapon almost as important as guns.

When you think of Hollywood in wartime, you can think of Bob Hope, Abbott and Cos-tello, Carole Lombard, Captain Clark Gable, Lieutenant Commander Robert Montgomery, Brigadier General Jimmy Stewart, Bette Davis of the Hollywood Canteen, Dorothy Lamour and all the other troupers who never faltered from a chance to serve.

The Hollywood Canteen, co-founded by Bette Davis and John Garfield, offered service-men on furlough a break from the war, a chance to relax, even to forget. Where better to unwind than Hollywood?

The fantasy capital offered a real nightclub where any GI Joe could dance with film's most glamorous actresses—including June Lang and Marlene Dietrich—and where major actors like Gary Cooper and Basil Rathbone rolled up their sleeves and pitched in for the sake of deserving soldiers and sailors.

Yes, it was a special time for Hollywood. Through four years of war, thousands of reels of film, endless hours at the Canteen, and USO tours in every corner of the world, it was Holly-wood's finest hour. ❖

Bob Hope is pictured with Frances Langford in a USO tour performance in World War II, around 1944. The show was also being broadcast over radio.

Bob Hope and the USO

Before and after World War II, Bob Hope was one of America's premier entertainers. However, it was dur-ing the war that this dedicated comedian gave his most appreciated and finest shows. Hope joined numerous musicians, actors and actresses who freely gave their time and talent to entertain the men and women in the service on stages all over the world.

These tours were no picnic; some, in fact, were extremely hazardous. Hope and his entourage found themselves in more than one sticky situation in the course of their hazardous globe-hopping. Hope's company sometimes performed perilously close to the front lines of action. But if our American troops could not go to a down-town movie theater in the United States to see Hope, he was determined to visit them—even if it meant traversing the globe during wartime and putting himself in some dangerous spots to do so.

When Bob Hope returned home after one 1940s European tour, he wrote an interesting, funny book, *I Never Left Home*. And in typical Hope fashion, he donated the royalties to the National War Fund. ❖

We Fought the War Too

Chapter Three

Malaysia is a long way from the central part of the United States of America—about 10,000 miles to be exact. Who would have thought that military incursions in this portion of Southeast Asia would have a profound effect in the lives of youngsters in the Western Hemisphere? But yet they did.

John Dinan remembers the World War II era as a time of sacrifice for everyone on the home front. In September 2001, John's story, "Use It Up, Wear It Out" was published in *Good Old Days* magazine and illustrated how the war affected the children of that generation:

"It isn't very often that world events directly affect a kid's life, but that's what happened after the Japanese attack on Pearl Harbor. There were shortages of items like shoes, meat, coffee, sugar, bicycles, etc.

"But even more importantly, there were shortages of strategic war materials, especially the tin and rubber produced by Japanese-controlled Malaysia.

"As a result of these shortages, two major movements occurred: home-front rationing, and scrap drives aimed at replenishing the basic materials of war.

"The Office of Price Administration (OPA) instituted price controls and rationing, and backed it up with patriotic slogans, reminding American civilians of their obligations, and that any sacrifices they made paled in comparison to what 'our boys' were doing on the battlefield.

We believed, and rightfully so, that scrap would win the war.

"On the radio, Bing Crosby sang *Junk Will Win the War* and encouraged citizens to donate their toothpaste tubes, scrap metal, bacon grease and other fats, and tin cans so that 'our boys' would not find themselves short of ammunition and the weapons of war.

"Kids were encouraged to gather these materials in door-to-door collections sponsored by neighborhood groups and the Boy Scouts. For the first time in our young lives, we could see a direct relationship between what we were doing and world affairs.

"It was a very heady experience for us kids as we set out on our Columbia bikes with balloon tires (if we had been lucky enough to have a bike when the war broke out) to collect scrap.

"Some of us rode in the back of a collection truck as it scoured the neighborhood for the likes of used tires, and aluminum pots and pans.

"We believed, and rightfully so, that scrap would win the war.

"According to Boy Scout statistics, the Scouts alone were responsible for collecting 109 million pounds of old rubber and 370 million pounds of scrap metal for the war effort.

"When the Japanese cut off our rubber and tin supplies from Malaysia in 1941, little did they think that America's kids would make up the difference."

So, our troops were fighting the war, but they weren't alone. Whether it was mothers, grandparents or, yes, even us kids—we fought the war too!

—Ken Tate

V Is for Veggies

By Hugh Neeld

"An indispensable source of food"—that's what the victory gardens were called in World War II. They were that, all right, but to me they were something more. I was in the sixth grade in 1941, and I remember hearing President Franklin Roosevelt on the radio, announcing that we were at war with Japan. I didn't have the foggiest notion of what that meant or where on earth Japan was. If there was anything taught in the Fort Worth public schools about Japan, I was either absent that day or not paying attention.

However, from my parents' reaction, I did know that this was something of more than passing importance. There was even a feeling of excitement about the whole thing. I tried to talk to my little brother about it, but he was even more clueless than I was.

Over the next few weeks, I began to get an idea of the changes in our lives that would be made by World War II. One change was that I started listening to news on the radio—a first for someone whose radio listening had been limited to *The Lone Ranger* and *I Love a Mystery*.

Our dinner table was a veritable cornucopia of vegetables.

Suddenly things were in short supply, and I learned a new word: *rationing*. And we'd thought the Depression was tough! All kinds of things were rationed—gasoline, cigarettes and canned goods, to name a few. Everyone accepted the fact that sacrifice was part of the deal and that we had to pitch in and do our part for the war effort.

Consolidated Aircraft—"the bomber plant," as it was called—was hiring women to work the assembly line. Yes, *women*! There was even a song about it: *Rosie the Riveter*. My mother, a housewife all her adult life, worked at the Army's Quartermaster Depot. People bought war bonds, conserved raw materials, recycled, rallied behind the troops and planted victory gardens.

For those too young to remember, victory gardens were a household activity on the home front designed to relieve pressure on the food supply. They were planted anywhere a few square feet of ground could be found: yards, parks, playgrounds, vacant lots—anywhere! Some 20 million victory gardens were grown, providing about 40 percent of the vegetables produced in the United States. By the end of the war, more than a million tons of vegetables had been grown, valued at $85 million.

It was a different time. The world had experienced more than a decade of economic hardship, and now people were being asked to give up more. The propaganda machine was geared up to make sure that

Facing page: *"V" Is for Victory Garden* by John Slobodnik © House of White Birches nostalgia archives

everyone on the home front did their part to help in the effort. The messages were simple, symbolic and patriotic.

Besides helping the war effort, victory gardens were morale boosters. Not only did people feel that they were making a major contribution to the war effort, but they were rewarded by growing their own produce. Victory gardens became a part of daily life. Emphasis was placed on making gardening a family or community effort— not a drudgery, but a national duty.

My brother and I worked hard to accept the "not a drudgery, but a national duty" part, but working in the garden after a hard day at school, plus a heavy-duty shift on Saturday, left little time for play. After my first full day in the garden under a hot summer sun, I looked more like a boiled lobster than a barefoot boy with cheeks of tan.

Although the government provided booklets that taught the basics of gardening, they assumed nobody knew anything about it and presented material accordingly. Like many of the adults on our block, my parents had been raised in large families living in rural areas. They were well schooled in when, where, what and how to plant. They were in their element. They *loved* it.

Our garden, shared by five other families on our block, was in a vacant lot next to our house. It was planted with every kind of vegetable that would grow in the Southwest: beans, beets, broccoli, brussels sprouts, cabbage, carrots, cauliflower, corn, cucumbers, eggplant, endive, leeks, lettuce, okra, onions, parsley, parsnips,

YOUR VICTORY GARDEN
counts more than ever!

War Food Administration poster, House of White Birches nostalgia archives

peas, peppers, radishes, rutabagas, spinach, squash, tomatoes and turnips.

Our dinner table was a veritable cornucopia of vegetables, some of which I never developed a taste for. I still experience a gag reflex when I hear the words *turnips* and *rutabagas*.

I will admit, though, that gardening was a great way to get acquainted with the neighbors and meet girls. As a matter of fact, that's where I met my first sweetheart, a petite, blue-eyed blonde with braces.

There's no telling how many pounds of vegetables that garden produced during the war, but the longer-lasting value to us was the friendships that resulted from working with our neighbors for a common cause— that, and of course, the memories.

When the war ended, so did the government's push for citizens to grow their own food. A lot of people felt it was a policy that was dropped too quickly.

These concepts are foreign to us today. After years of economic growth and marketing messages promoting consumerism, generations of young people know no other way. As the population ages, we lose the experience and knowledge gained during the Depression and World War II.

History is cyclical. The strong economy of the past two decades has begun to weaken, and there are lessons to be learned from the past. Now might be a good time to plant your own victory garden. A quote from Henry Ford comes to mind: "No unemployment insurance can be compared to an alliance between man and a plot of land." ❖

Mom's Gardens

By Helen Patton Gray

We called them "victory gardens" during World War II. Anyone who had land enough to plant even a few rows of vegetables was encouraged to do so. That was partly due to the shortage of agricultural labor, since so many young men had been drafted or volunteered for the armed services.

There was a vacant lot next to our home in Kansas City, Mo., that "nobody" seemed to own, so it served as our victory garden during the war years. Every spring, Mom donned a pair of work gloves, put a bandanna scarf on her head, and then grabbed a spade, rake and hoe to turn the soil before the weeds began to sprout. We had fresh vegetables each summer, as well as canned tomatoes, carrots and green beans all winter long, along with pickled beets and dill pickles.

Mom asked for minimal help from other family members in tending her crops. She had lived on a farm much of her life, so gardening was not an unusual task for her. I did get to help by fetching Mason jars, pulling the skins off the scalded tomatoes and cleaning up the kitchen when the day's canning was done.

In addition to the vegetable gardens, Mom always planted rows of flowers in front of her veggies, as a camouflage to shield her agricultural accomplishments from street traffic. In those days, people wouldn't snatch snapdragons, zinnias, petunias, marigolds or daisies, but the vegetables would tempt some.

Looking back, I remember the climate in Missouri as being ideal for growing things from seed planted directly in the soil. If rain didn't provide enough moisture, the garden hose was there for sprinkling. Sunny days and cool evenings back then were ideal for planting and harvesting.

When the war ended, it also brought to an end the victory garden era. My brothers came home from the service, married within a year, and then left the area. Mom stopped planting her gardens, and a new home was built on the vacant lot. Things had changed forever in the neighborhood. The beautiful old elm trees that lined our street were cut down due to Dutch elm disease, and not too many years later, a freeway wiped out all the homes and left many blocks of Montgall Avenue a thing of the past.

I also left Kansas City, and now I live in Wisconsin. However, I always think of Mom when I do my spring planting. In Wisconsin, very few flower gardens are started from seed, but the garden shops offer an array of blooming plants, waiting to be cared for and enjoyed.

While tending to my petunias and impatiens, I am reminded of how Mom used her magic touch during all those summers to provide pretty flowers in her garden. Now I realize that it wasn't the farmer in her; it was her love of beauty and her desire to share it with family, neighbors and passersby. ❖

Rationing Recipes

By Winnie Rhoades Schuetz

The other day I bought an old cookbook at a yard sale, and as I paged through it, I found a pamphlet entitled "Recipes to Stretch Your Sugar Ration." The pamphlet was dated 1942 and had been put out by Church & Dwight, makers of Arm & Hammer baking soda. As I looked through it, I remembered my mother using honey, molasses and corn syrup to stretch her sugar. We liked jelly and preserves, and Mom worked hard to save our sugar to make those items.

Sugar rationing was one of the limitations we had to live with during World War II. We also had gasoline rationing, meat rationing and difficulty getting tires. It wasn't long before my dad put his car up on blocks and rode to work with a neighbor, sharing his gasoline points in exchange for the ride. He often helped that neighbor work on his car, too, and a couple of times, he helped pay for a part from the junkyard. New parts were scarce.

We soon got used to making do with what we had when we couldn't get what we were used to. We were much more fortunate than people in the city; we had chickens, and we got our milk from a nearby farmer. And we grew a huge garden before victory gardens became popular. We sold our produce door-to-door in town. That helped pay our taxes and electric bill until my dad got a job in a war plant.

My dad was too old to go to war, so he helped make things that went to war. Even though he worked long hours, he still found time to take care of things at home.

The war years were hard on everyone. On the home front, we all did our part. Kids bought stamps at school to fill books that could be turned in for war bonds. By the time the war was over, I had five $25 bonds.

I got $1.25 a week for doing my chores and keeping up my grades. I had to save the dollar, but the quarter was mine to spend. That required

Ration stamps were needed to buy necessities such as shoes, sugar, coffee, meat, flour and eggs.

careful thought every Saturday. I loved comic books, and I bought one every week for 10 cents.

Besides my allowance, my dad used to give me a quarter to go to the show. He said a person should have a little fun after working hard. So I went to the show every Saturday. Admission was a dime, and I could get popcorn, candy and a soda pop, each for a nickel. Think what that costs today!

I lived in a town with an Army camp nearby, so I was used to seeing soldiers all the time. When friends came to visit from out of town, they gawked at the men in uniform. My cousin was stationed there, and some of the young soldiers came with him to visit us. We usually had a good time on Friday and Saturday nights.

One Saturday night, my cousin and some of the GIs were practicing their *jujitsu* in our front yard. The neighbors thought they were brawling and called the law. Next thing we knew, we saw lights coming down the road. When the soldiers explained, the sheriff laughed all the way to the squad car.

I was only 7 years old when Japan bombed Pearl Harbor. That was a bad day for our country, but it brought prosperity in the form of jobs. Then, due to shortages, we couldn't buy a lot of things. But we learned to adjust to a new way of living.

My mother was always experimenting with ways to cook things within the rationing rules. Some of her experiments turned out mighty well. I loved her sugar cookies made with honey, and I still asked for them even when we could get all the sugar we wanted.

Back in those pre-war years, it was the style for kids to snack on butter bread with sugar sprinkled on top. But I didn't miss the sugar on my bread because I liked straight honey.

However, I did love potatoes fried in bacon grease, and I asked Mom to hold enough bacon grease back from the grease can we saved so

The author at age 9, in 1943.

that we could have a treat now and then. She usually did.

All us kids saved tinfoil. We competed to see who could accumulate the biggest ball. Dad had all his smoking friends save the foil from their packages for me, and I ended up with one of the largest balls brought in. My dad usually rolled his own, so I didn't get much tinfoil from him.

During those war years, we listened to the radio every night. We never missed the news or our favorite programs. I listened to my favorites after school. Who could miss *Captain Midnight* and *Terry and the Pirates*? But I really had to hurry with my chores to get in the house in time. Sometimes Mom let me bring in the coal and water after supper.

My all-time favorite program was broadcast on Saturday morning. When I heard the Cream of Wheat theme, I knew it was time for *Let's Pretend*, a program of dramatized fairy tales.

During the 1930s and '40s, our main entertainment was the radio. Women listened to "soap operas"; my mom liked *Aunt Jenny, Ma Perkins, Stella Dallas, Our Gal Sunday* and *One Man's Family*. I also listened to them when I was sick and stayed home from school.

Our whole family listened to *Amos and Andy* over WMAQ from Chicago, as well as *Fibber McGee and Molly*. WMAQ had a very strong signal, reaching out all over the country. We also loved Red Skelton, Sherlock Holmes and Charlie Chan.

Those war years were often sad as well as difficult, but we managed to get through them. Certainly we were glad to see peace come again. It was a real relief when we were once again able to buy as much meat and gas as we needed, as well as a new car. And sugar … I was glad that I again could be sure of a good supply of Mom's strawberry preserves, my favorite. ❖

Rationing Was a Way of Life

By Kathy Manney

I was born in Portland, Ore., in March 1942—three months after America entered World War II. With two major tributaries, the Willamette and Columbia rivers, Portland was a bustling port and bridge city, and it remains so to this day. Gas, sugar, flour, meat, fish, cheese, fats and canned goods all were rationed, but the war effort only heightened everyone's resourcefulness. And though there were nationwide shortages and rationing, we didn't want for too many things.

Being the firstborn daughter, granddaughter and niece, I was enveloped in love and nurturing. When I grew and needed new shoes, there was always someone in our household willing to give up her shoe ration for me. Portland's daily morning newspaper, *The Oregonian*, printed a rationing calendar for its readers. It suggested readers attach the calendar "to your ration book for convenience," and Grandma did just that.

My earliest memories are of living in a household of three working women—Mom, my aunt and my paternal grandmother, all of whom worked in defense plants, building ships for wartime. Today's safety standards were nonexistent, and it was hard and sometimes dangerous work.

World War II broke down the barriers that had previously kept women from holding many positions. Now, with most of America's young men fighting overseas, the demand for workers promptly allowed women to overcome the challenge of gender discrimination.

In those Good Old Days, women were the army on the home front. Back then, it seemed normal to see women working in occupations formerly monopolized by men. Our mail carrier was a woman, as were many of Portland's public transit

From "Seaside to where THE YANKS are winning!" The author's Aunt Mildred posed during a beach vacation so she could send the photo to her husband, who was fighting in the Pacific in 1943.

drivers. Instead of a milkman, we had a "milk lady." And Oregon called the first women to jury duty in federal court in 1942, when minimum wage was 43 cents per hour.

Besides Mom and Aunt Mildred, both my grandmothers held jobs that contributed to the war effort. My paternal grandmother, with whom we shared a home, was a steel burner in one of the area's three shipyards. My maternal grandmother was a nurse at the Veteran's Hospital in nearby Vancouver, Wash.

In those days, our nation's resources were committed to supporting our troops around the world. Victory gardening was encouraged so that more food could be sent overseas.

Soon after my maternal grandmother was hired at the Veteran's Hospital, she bought a small, white frame house on a large lot with a full lot adjoining it. It was perfect for her plans to sow a sizable "garden for victory." Grandma worked the swing shift at the hospital, which allowed her time during the day to work the soil around her house. She grew large quantities of vegetables and fruits for herself, family and friends. Artificial fertilizers were unavailable, but Grandma saved lawn clippings and table scraps for composting.

Sometimes Aunt Mildred liked to pretend I was her little girl, and she would take me downtown shopping with her. Other times I would accompany both Mom and Aunt Mildred, and they would take me to lunch at Meier & Frank, a locally owned department store.

Back then, going shopping was something you dressed for. Women wore high heels, hats and gloves; even little girls like me wore dresses, hats and gloves to travel downtown. At Meier & Frank, we would eat in the Tea Room. Today, more than 70 years after it opened, the elegant Georgian Tea Room is still a Portland landmark.

These ration stamps (top and bottom) were affixed inside the author's grandmother's brown ration book.

As a child, I was fascinated by the trolley bus and how, at the end of the line, the driver would call, "End of the line!" then walk to the opposite end of the car and start the trolley back the way we had come. The clatter of trolleys was once a familiar sound in Portland. At one time the city had more than 250 miles of trolley tracks crisscrossing the city. We lived a few blocks from the trolley and streetcar lines. In those days, riders mingled in friendly fashion as they waited at the stops.

Trolleys, trolley buses and streetcars were the wheels on which the city traveled in the Good Old Days. With wartime gasoline rationing, most

Portlanders used public transportation. Street-cars were a handy way to move large numbers of people, and they carried many passengers to work, to shopping downtown and on pleasure outings.

Portland's landmark Union Station with its 140-foot clock tower served five passenger lines and 4.8 million people during World War II with 74 trains running daily. From the time I was a toddler, Mom and I were travel companions during her vacations from the shipyard.

In the summertime, we visited the town of Seaside, 80 miles west of Portland, on the beautiful Oregon coast. I played in the sand and on the swings whose sturdy frames had been installed near the oceanfront promenade with its historic automobile turnaround and spectacular ocean view. This was the center of Seaside's activity. Visitors could rent trikes and bikes to ride along the promenade. There was also a fancy carousel nearby for "horsey rides."

Those turbulent wartime days brought hardships, shortages and rationing. But many remember them as a time of change and independence for women. Mom and Aunt Mildred are great-grandmothers in their 80s now, and they fondly recall the time when they were young sisters-in-law and close friends, living and working together.

There was no "women's lib" then; Mom, Aunt Mildred and my grandmothers weren't trying to be trailblazers when they worked in occupations that supported the war effort. It was just something that happened, and they simply seized the opportunities that opened for them. Everywhere there was an atmosphere of determination, of trying to make the best of things.

Little did Mom and my aunt know that while they were working and pooling their ration stamps so that we could all enjoy a better standard of living during a time of unequivocal shortages, they were also building a store of memories, both for themselves and for the little girl they both treated as their own. ❖

Above: The author (center) with her mother (left) and Aunt Mildred (right) are all dressed up on their day off from the shipyard. Hats and gloves were the order of the day for downtown shopping in 1944. They pooled their shoe ration stamps to keep the author in white high-top shoes. Below: Mileage stickers were required to be displayed on all vehicles. "A" indicated nonessential use. "T" stickers were issued for trucks and commercial vehicles. Government vehicles, police and fire were given "X" stickers which indicated unlimited use and larger allocations of fuel.

THIS STICKER MUST BE DISPLAYED ON THE VEHICLE ONLY IN THAT LOCATION WHICH CONFORMS WITH THE STATE LAW

To Save Tires Drive Under 35

✓ Share your car
✓ Check air pressure weekly
✓ Stop, start, turn slowly
✓ Cross-switch tires regularly

Is This Trip Really Necessary?

A

MILEAGE RATION

The Unlocked Door

By Douglas A. Nielsen

No one expected the door to a store to be unlocked at night—especially since the store was a butcher shop. It was 1943, and World War II was in high gear.   Meat was expensive and rationed. Anyone finding a butcher store unlocked would be sorely tempted to empty the store and have meat for weeks—provided he had an extra freezer, of course.

Dad was a Civil Defense volunteer. He and his partner were on patrol that night. They were wearing their uniforms and sidearms as they patrolled the streets of Tottenville, Staten Island. I was pretty proud of Dad because he was authorized to carry that gun. It didn't occur to me that a lot more was entrusted to him than that firearm.

As Dad and his partner walked down the row of stores, they checked doors and looked into windows to be sure that all was well. When they reached Mr. Sorenson's butcher shop and checked the door, it was open. Dad's partner agreed to stay at the door while Dad went to Mr. Sorenson's house. He planned to bring Mr. Sorenson to the store to lock up. But that was easier said than done.

When Dad knocked on the front door, there was no reply, though there was a light on in the house. He knocked again, and looking through the etched-glass door, he could see the Sorensons

RATIONING MEANS A FAIR SHARE FOR ALL OF US

WITHOUT RATIONING

WITH RATIONING

World War II Office of Price Administration poster, House of White Birches nostalgia archives

down the hallway in their kitchen. Mr. Sorenson acted as though he hadn't heard a thing. Again Dad knocked; still no response.

Now, Dad was over 6 feet tall and about 190 pounds, a carpenter by trade. He was beginning to get a little perturbed. A fourth time he knocked, this time with considerable force. Finally, Mr. Sorenson came to the door, obviously upset with the insistent knocking.

As soon as he saw Dad, he asked what was wrong. Dad explained his shop door was open, and he'd better come and lock it. Mr. Sorenson got his keys and accompanied Dad to the store.

On the way, he apologized for not answering the door sooner. He explained that almost every night, someone would come and try to get meat without ration stamps. He had been offered large sums of money to sell meat illegally and would not do it. He thought Dad was a would-be black-market customer.

When they got to the shop, everything was in order; nothing had been stolen. Mr. Sorenson had forgotten to lock the front door when he went out the back. When he locked up, all three checked the door. Mr. Sorenson went home after a number of thank-yous, and Dad and his partner continued their patrol. I thought it would have been nice if Mr. Sorenson had rewarded Dad with a steak or a half-dozen chops, but it was wartime, and meat was rationed. ❖

My Bike Won the War

By Bob Griggs

It was 1943. I was only 13 years old, but I knew about the war. I was a paperboy, delivering the *Oregon Journal* in Portland, Ore. Every day I read the major stories before starting my route. I wished I could help our side, but I was just a kid. Most of the other boys had bicycles. I didn't; I carried my papers on foot—and I had a double route that started 10 blocks from the paper station. Those papers were heavy, especially on Sundays. I needed a bicycle, but this was wartime. Adults needed bicycles because gasoline was rationed; kids' needs were less important.

John Drew

Still, I had hope. That hope was finally realized one day when my dad came home with a real bicycle. It wasn't new; it had no fenders, and in fact, it was pretty old, but the tires were OK. And it was painted red.

Boy, was it *red*—and the paint was new, so new that it was still tacky in places. I didn't know where Dad found it, but he'd paid 10 whole dollars for it, practically a fortune in those times.

The next day, I pedaled down to the paper station. I rolled up my papers, and with the bag hanging from the handlebars, I was off to my route. It was pretty keen. It took a few days to get my aim and timing perfected, but I did, and without breaking any windows or screen doors.

About a week later, though, disaster struck. A tree root had pushed up a section of cement sidewalk. I hit it; something went *snap!* and my bike started to wobble. I got off and looked. The place where the back fork joined the pedal crank housing had separated. I could see that the original weld had broken before, but instead of welding it back, the former owner had soldered it. It hadn't held when I hit the bump—but it did help explain all that fresh red paint.

Dad was as griped as I was. He'd been taken, and the guy from whom he'd bought the bike had vanished. There weren't many shops in our area where he could get it fixed, but he did work out a temporary repair with a small turnbuckle. It sort of solved the problem as long as I was careful, but it sure took the joy out of my paper route.

That's when the war entered my life. Across the street from the paper station, a large building had been torn down. All that was left was the basement, and that was now being used to collect scrap-metal for the war effort. A sign there explained that the metal would be melted down and made into airplanes and tanks for the war.

I was pretty impressed. Dad had an old bucket with holes in the bottom. I filled it with all the metal stuff I could find that we didn't need and lugged it down to the donation spot and dumped it over the side. There were all sorts of things down there: old bed springs, car parts, water tanks, everything you could imagine, including an old, rusty bicycle frame! That's when I got my big idea.

Risking my life, I climbed down and managed to untangle the bike frame from the rest of the junk. As near as I could tell, it was almost like my red wreck of a bike.

I rushed through my route that evening and then sneaked back to the scrap-metal basement and dragged the bike frame home, where I hid it in the little garage that was too small for Dad's car. It took me more than a week, and the judicious use of Dad's tools, but I managed to switch all of the parts from the red bike over to my new find. It worked, it really worked! I wasn't stealing from the war effort, I told myself as I dragged the red frame back to the basement and dropped it in; I was just trading.

I wasn't stealing from the war effort ... I was just trading.

Later Dad and I met when I was coming back from running my paper route. "Didn't that bike used to be red?" he asked. "And what happened to the turnbuckle?"

"Oh, I ... uh ... *fixed* it," I said. "Well, I gotta go now!" And I pedaled off, leaving him scratching his head.

I guess my dad must have been a genius or something, because about six months later, I came home to find a brand-new bike on the front porch. It was a big delivery bike with a huge basket over a small front wheel, and it was red also—not barn red this time, but more like ripe cherries. It was magnificent. Dad and I made a deal that I would pay for half from my paper route.

Boy, was I the envy of the other guys at the paper station! I could put all my papers in that basket, even the Sunday ones. And, you ask, what did I do with my other hybrid bicycle?

I sold the tires and inner tubes to one kid for 50 cents and the seat to another for a dime; the rest went back into the scrap-metal collection and eventually went off to win the war. I felt pretty patriotic about that. ❖

Lining Up for Nylons

By Arthur Jackson

"**A**rthur, are you doing anything special today?" Ardelle asked as I entered the kitchen. It was a Saturday, and as far as I could see, the day was blissfully free.

"Not that I know of. It's Saturday."

"I know it's Saturday," she purred, "and I'd like to ask a tiny favor."

I turned to look her straight in the eye, and I could do that now. Ardelle was nine years older, as she'd been pointing out for as long as I could remember. But lately I'd come to realize that I was a bit taller than she—a point I was quick to remind her of frequently.

"You're just the dearest, sweetest little brother a girl could have."

Uh-oh, I thought. *What am I getting myself into?* "What?" I asked.

Her smile was sweet. "National Shoes has a shipment of nylons in, and they're going on sale today."

> *"I want two pairs of stockings for my sister," I stated bravely.*

"Nylons? You mean like socks?"

"Stockings, dear," she corrected gently. "My schedule is packed full already today, and I don't have an extra minute to go downtown. If you're willing to go for me, you can have a whole dollar for your own."

Well now, *that* didn't sound so bad. It was a 20-block walk from our home in Jamaica, N.Y., to National Shoes. A long walk on a beautiful day like this was a real treat for me. Plus, I really did want to help Ardelle out. She was planning to wear those socks on her Saturday-night date. And the promised dollar was a pure bonus.

I breathed a sigh of relief. "I thought you wanted something hard. Of course I'll go get your socks … stockings." I grinned at her.

She dug a $5 bill out of her purse. "They cost $2 for each pair, and you know what to do with the other dollar." She handed me the bill with a sly wink. I felt rich as I made my way up the street to Jamaica Avenue with Ardelle's money safely tucked into my pocket.

Funny, I thought, *that stockings should be so hard to get. Just a couple years ago you could buy stuff like that whenever you needed it, without waiting for a special shipment.*

Other things had changed too. Gasoline, sugar, meat, butter—many such items were now rationed, and others were scarce, not that anyone seemed to mind. We knew it was all for the war effort. Even shoes had changed. When we could get them at all, they were usually made of flimsy materials. *They sure don't wear as well as before,* I thought as I scuffed down the long street. Good furniture, appliances and radios were all hard to find now.

We even had "blackout" drills at school and neighborhood wardens providing defense suggestions for our homes in case of attack or other emergencies. A lot had changed since that day no one could forget: Dec. 7, 1941.

As I got closer to downtown, things got more interesting. I crossed Liberty Avenue and went under the Long Island Railroad tracks. Ahead I saw the elevated tracks of the BMT, a part of the rapid-transit system that served many boroughs of New York City. Then there was Gurtz, the town's leading department store, and Woolworths, and then, at the corner of 161st and Jamaica Avenue, was the National Shoe store.

Rationing caused many lines at stores in World War II, like this on captured in 1943. Photo courtesy the U.S. National Archives.

When I was about a block away, I saw something that brought me to a standstill. A long, restless line of humanity had formed, stretching from the doorway most of the way to the corner. Why was there such a long line at that store?

My heart dropped all the way to my heels as I realized the answer to my own question. Every person in that line was after the same thing I was after—nylons. Hmmm. This was going to be harder than I'd thought.

I meekly took my place at the end of the line, which crept forward for maybe an hour before I actually entered the store. At last I stood at the head of the line, facing a tired-looking clerk.

"How may I help you, son?" she asked. I hated being called "son."

"I want two pairs of stockings for my sister," I stated bravely.

She eyed me cautiously. "I think you mean nylon stockings," she said with emphasis. She picked up a box. "What size does she wear?"

Whoa! Wait a minute! Ardelle hadn't said a word about her size! How was I supposed to know? I tried to be cool. "Oh, probably just the usual size." I waited for a response, but got none. "Her shoes are not very big." Suddenly I had an idea. "She's not very big. Oh, she's a grown-up, but she didn't grow up much. Now I'm as tall as she is, and I'm only 14," I finished hopefully.

By now I was hearing restless murmurs from the line behind me. I saw a hint of a smile at the corners of the clerk's firmly set lips.

"Well, that might help us some," she said grudgingly. "Now, what color does she want?"

I sure wasn't prepared for that one, either. I gulped, "Aren't they mostly just brownish?"

"Actually, they vary from light to darker shades. You should have asked your sister."

Again I heard murmurings behind me. Clearly I was taking too long. Well, we'd come this far; I wouldn't turn back now. "Just give me the usual color, whatever most customers like."

She selected another box and placed them on the counter. "Based on the information I have, this is the best I can do," she sighed. "If she doesn't like them, maybe she can trade them for something else." A relieved sigh whispered through the line behind me. I handed her that money and pocketed the extra dollar. I had earned that prize!

I sure hoped Ardelle would be happy with the nylons we had chosen for her. I knew I would never go through that ordeal again, so she'd *better* like them. Besides, she needed to wear them tonight. She'd *have* to like them.

I thought I might stop at Woolworth's to squander my dollar, but I decided to wait. I'd struggled with enough decisions for one day.

The restrictions of World War II are but a memory now. Ardelle continued to be a satisfied customer of National Shoes. And I was glad to let her do her own shopping there! ❖

Our Essex

By Mrs. Ralph Lindsay

The year was 1942. Shaken and shocked by the sneak attack at Pearl Harbor, we had no idea where the next attack on the United States would take place. On the West Coast, we felt particularly vulnerable.

The manufacture of civilian goods ceased, and factories converted to producing war materials. Automobiles, appliances, leather shoes, meat, sugar, coffee and canned goods were among rationed items. We could not travel by train or bus, as these were reserved for troop transport.

But we desperately wanted to help the war effort. We volunteered as air-raid wardens and plane spotters; we organized USO canteens, knitted sweaters, and coordinated scrap-metal and rubber drives. Japan now controlled most of the world's rubber, tin and copper. We joked bitterly that all the scrap iron Japan had purchased from us for years was now being returned as bombs!

My husband managed a service station in San Bernardino, Calif. You remember service stations, where someone pumped your gas, checked your oil, battery and tires, and cleaned your windshield and windows. All this, and gasoline was 20 cents a gallon. During the war, these stations also served as collection points for the scrap drive. As you can imagine, people did

not throw away a tire that could be useful.

To my husband's surprise, a man brought in four almost-new tires for the drive. He said he had taken them off an old car in his backyard. Furthermore, he told my husband, he would give the car to anyone who would haul it away. With no prospects of being able to buy a car anytime soon, we decided to accept his offer.

When my husband went to get the car, he found a 1929 Essex up on blocks, almost completely hidden by weeds and grass, and covered by dust so thick that he could not tell its color. With the help of some friends, he took the car to a garage. After steam-cleaning, scrubbing, dusting and polishing, the old car turned out to be dark green with leather upholstery in good condition, wooden wheels and four almost-new tires. She carried us in comfort for the rest of the war.

She did have several idiosyncrasies, however. Every 50 miles, we had to stop and kick the rear right wheel—it kept slipping off. Her top speed was 50 mph, and the overflow cup filled with rust after each trip. But she rode majestically above the crowd, like the *Queen Mary* in a sea of rowboats. Our cat loved to sleep on the cloth roof, and we often had to stop and remove her down the road. But above all, we felt safe, and she lasted until the war ended. ❖

Rationing at the A&P

By LaVerne Fieseler

As I pushed my grocery cart through the supermarket this morning and viewed the wide array of choices, my mind drifted back to the small A&P where my mother shopped in the 1940s. Choices and quantities were limited not only by wartime rationing, but also by the lack of technology and marketing techniques.

Rationing was needed so that we could send vital food and other products overseas to our fighting troops. As I remember, among the items rationed were tires, soap, gas, cigarettes, butter, sugar, meat and coffee.

Ration coupons were issued so that people would not hoard more than they needed. The size of the family determined how many ration coupons each family received. There were coupons for meat, coffee, sugar, gas, tires and other staples.

Neighbors sometimes traded ration coupons for items they needed more than others. We never drank coffee, so my mother traded our coffee coupons to our childless neighbor for sugar coupons or soap coupons, which she didn't need so badly.

Rubber was scarce too. As a result, tires resembled patchwork quilts. Our 20-mile Saturday-morning trip to the grocery store—if we had our allotted gallon of gas—could well include two or three stops to fix a flat with another "boot." And as for steel—ever hear of a 1944 Ford or Chevy? No? None were built during the war years. No cars were manufactured here for several years during World War II so the steel could be used to build tanks and jeeps, and to manufacture ammunition instead.

There was no chocolate, and—even worse for me—no toys were manufactured during the war. I did receive a Shirley Temple doll, which my mother found at a rummage sale and bought for 10 cents. But the doll's hair had been cut off by the previous "rich girl" owner.

Even the soap powder we used to wash our clothes was rationed. (We called it "soap" back then; we'd never heard of "detergent.") Our local A&P would set out a large carton of Rinso or Oxydol at 9 o'clock each morning and a swarm of housewives would swoop down on it. The carton was empty in seconds. But to prevent hoarding, each housewife was allowed only one box. My mother was a heavy-set woman and couldn't wiggle her way to the carton, so I crawled under the scrambling housewives and grabbed a box.

Fortunately, we lived in a rural area and raised chickens, so we usually had plenty of meat. Fried chicken, stewed chicken, roasted chicken, chicken potpie, chicken, chicken, chicken. It's no wonder I can barely look at chicken now.

And since sugar was in short supply, I learned to eat foods like cold cereal and oatmeal without it.

And since sugar was in short supply, I learned to eat foods like cold cereal and oatmeal without it. To this day, I don't put sugar on anything.

Butter was another luxury. This was when oleomargarine came into its own. Margarine did not come in yellow sticks as it does today. Back then, margarine was white. But people complained that it looked like they were spreading lard on their bread, so a little packet of yellow dye was included with the margarine. We mixed the contents of the dye packet into the margarine sticks and stored them in the refrigerator.

All the nylon was needed for parachutes, leaving none for ladies' nylon stockings. Instead, ladies used tan-colored lotion on their legs to give the appearance of stockings.

Yes, those were the days of rationing, but we didn't mind. We gladly did without. Our sacrifices helped win World War II! ❖

Serious Recycling

By Robert J. Miller

Recycling is in vogue today as a means of preserving the environment, but it really flourished during World War II, when the war years saw America's urban civilians recycling in a big way—not just to aid the military effort, but also to support the economy of the home front. Serious recycling gained impetus from a growing shortage of natural rubber following the swift Japanese conquest of Southeast Asia, which was our principal source. President Roosevelt was prompted to institute a rubber reclamation program. He asked the nation's gas-station operators to act as collection points and implored the public to turn in all worn-out and unwanted auto tires and tubes, overshoes, hot-water bottles, hoses, floor mats and raincoats.

In a wave of patriotism, most everyone participated in the program, and processing plants were able to meet the needs of the Armed Forces. As a further incentive, the president authorized payment of 1 cent a pound for used rubber.

No consumer could purchase a new tube of toothpaste without turning in an empty.

At that time, toothpaste tubes were made of a metal alloy containing a lot of tin, which was also imported from Southeast Asia. In order to ensure a sufficient supply for packaging their product, dentifrice manufacturers stipulated that no consumer could purchase a new tube of toothpaste without turning in an empty.

We city dwellers participated in recycling in other mandated ways. When placing trash out for collection, we had to bundle all cardboard and paper, separate all glass and metal containers, and bag all cotton materials for transport to appropriate processing plants. Before setting them out at curbside, all tin cans had to be stripped of labels and washed; then the ends had to be removed and placed inside the flattened cans, which had to be bundled for ease of handling.

Large metal objects of iron, steel and aluminum were usually donated to the numerous scrap drives organized for the benefit of nonprofit entities like the Boy Scouts, Red Cross, Salvation Army, schools and churches. Nonferrous metals were often sold to the local junkyard, which became an important source of supply for many wartime endeavors.

Except for the ashes from the ubiquitous coal furnace, there was little household waste relegated to landfills. Even the ashes were sifted for bits of unburnt coal before being placed on the curb for collection, and in cold weather, they, too, were recycled when the

city workers spread them on slippery streets in place of scarce salt and sand.

Householders were encouraged to save the drippings of cooking oil, lard and fats for collection by the neighborhood butcher for transport to area rendering plants. Glycerins were extracted from the waste to make soap, gunpowder, solvents, resins and similar products.

Many store owners took advantage of the recycling craze to reduce their costs. They wrapped their goods in old newspapers and salvaged bags. Manufacturers and suppliers of goods bought used cardboard cartons from scrap dealers, turned the boxes inside out and placed fresh labels on them to use for shipping and storage. Unneeded labels were covered with paint before applying fresh ones.

Rationing was also the order of the times. The government established ration offices in each locality to which a family had to apply for permission to buy such necessities as shoes, sugar, coffee, meat, butter, flour and eggs. Allocations were made by use of stamps and certificates, and were based on family size, availability of supplies and occupation.

Generally, those engaged in hard manual labor related to the war effort, like shipyard or steel workers, were given extra rations, as were small children. Markets for substitute goods flourished, as did a "black market" where most anything could be purchased if one had the price.

Automobile owners were subject to a special set of rationing regulations. Need had to be proven. The basic ration of gasoline was three gallons

Advertisement from the Philadelphia Record, 1944. *Valid ration stamps are noted at the top of the ad.*

a week, but those engaged in essential occupations were given larger allocations. Each vehicle had to display a ration sticker with a letter designation identifying its use and gasoline allocation.

An "A" sticker indicated nonessential use and entitled the driver to the basic ration of just three gallons a week. In order to purchase the fuel, the drive had to present a dated ration stamp to the gas-station operator before refueling began.

"T" stickers were issued for trucks and other commercial vehicles, and carried larger allocations. Government vehicles, police cars, fire trucks and the like were given "X" stickers for unlimited use and the largest allocations of fuel.

Although it was illegal to do so, automobile owners soon learned that unused and unwanted ration stamps could be easily sold or traded, and passed off to unscrupulous gasoline dealers.

Even more so than gasoline, tires for all vehicles were in short supply. They could be purchased only for the most essential uses and only after vehicle owners convinced the authorities that a pressing need existed. While a certificate of need may have been issued, the vehicle owner was always faced with the problem of finding a tire dealer with a decent inventory. Most owners turned to the tire recapping shops, even though the quality of recaps was suspect.

As the war dragged on, car and truck owners faced another major problem—finding replacement parts. Parts manufacturers sent all their output to the Armed Forces, prompting auto owners to turn to the junkyards, where worn-out cars were stripped of all usable parts before being turned into scrap metal. Even so, there weren't enough parts around to meet the demand. Enterprising mechanics became adept at cannibalizing old equipment in order to keep cars in service. In the long run, however, most cars were eventually abandoned or stored away for the duration.

Wartime saw a proliferation of secondhand stores that bought, refurbished and sold household goods. Quality furniture and new appliances were virtually unattainable, even if one had the money, so every item in the home was used until the last bit of its life was expended. Worn-out clocks, radios, toasters and the like were stripped of all salvageable parts by used-goods merchants who recycled them into marketable wares.

Money was recycled too. To help finance the war effort, retailers were encouraged to purchase savings stamps, which were offered to customers in lieu of monetary change. The stamps were issued in various denominations, and many people accepted them, then inserted them in government-supplied booklets that were later turned in for defense bonds. Even schoolchildren were asked to take savings stamps in place of coins when buying their recess snacks and lunches.

In the early 1940s, recycling arrived in America with a vengeance that has not been equaled, even with today's emphasis on protecting the environment. Everything was reused one way or another, and we lived by the slogan promulgated by the government: "Use it up; wear it out; make it do; or do without." ❖

A Wing and a Prayer

By Mrs. Gilbert Patton

My sister-in-law and I took our children to a youth rally about 60 miles from home. I never gave the gas situation much thought. I just figured we had enough.

After the rally, on our way home, I glanced at the gas gauge and realized we were getting low. Gas stations didn't stay open late in those days because of rationing. We hoped to find one still open, but we didn't.

As we traveled on, I said, "Let's sing *Coming In on a Wing and a Prayer*." It was a very popular song at that time.

Yes, we made it home. But my car wouldn't start the next morning.

Fortunately, I had parked on the street. The street had a slight grade, so I was able to coast down to the gas station on the corner.

What a miracle! ❖

Wartime Ice Cream

By David D. Westerfield

In the fall of 1936, we moved from Galesburg, Ill., to the nearby hamlet of Knoxville. I spent my formative years in this small farming community. When World War II started, I was 7 years old. The war had an impact on our family of eight in many ways. But while there were shortages of many kinds, most didn't bother us much. Dad carpooled to his job at Midwest Manufacturing, which was 6 miles away, in Galesburg. His turn to drive came only every fourth week, so gas and tires were not a major problem.

We hunted and fished, so the meat shortage was not a problem, either. In fact, we raised most of what we ate. We harvested a variety of vegetables, canning them and storing them in the cellar along with potatoes, carrots, apples and pears. These lasted through the winter until we could raise more.

Sugar, however, was a problem. We needed it to preserve fruit—in jams and jellies, and whole for the table. And not only was sugar in short supply, but it was rationed. Sometimes we canned grape juice without sugar and added it later, when the need was not so great.

One of the casualties of the sugar rationing was ice cream.

Back then, people traded ration stamps like kids trade baseball cards. If you had an old clunker in the backyard that was still registered and got gas stamps, you could trade them for rides to work.

But everyone, it seemed, needed their sugar stamps. Our great-aunt lived next door. While she did a lot of baking, she usually had extra sugar stamps, which she shared with us. This helped, but we still were short, and our supply was managed carefully. One of the casualties of the sugar rationing was ice cream. Our family liked ice cream, but we just couldn't spare sugar for such frivolous things.

One day my Uncle Frannie, a farmer, mentioned that their peaches were ripe. We quite naturally concluded that we ought to make some peach ice cream. We had done without for a couple of years by now, and my folks and Uncle Frannie and Aunt Mildred decided that enough was enough. The peaches were ripe, and the best use one could make of peaches was in ice cream. So we were going to make some good old homemade ice cream!

On the appointed day, we gathered at Uncle Frannie's farm 4 miles east of town and 2 miles north of Gilson. This was "the old home place," where Mom's family all had grown up. We brought rock salt, the ice and our carefully hoarded sugar. The women prepared the peaches and cooked up a batch of ice cream using real cream.

Meanwhile, the men got out the mixer, cleaned it and got it ready to freeze. The can was filled with the precious contents. Then the lid was put on tight, and the can was placed in the freezer. The crank's gears were engaged and the crank was locked onto the can. The space between the walls of the can and the freezer was filled clear to the top with layers of ice and salt.

It was quite a festive atmosphere as we all took turns cranking or sitting on the freezer to hold it down. Dad added ice and salt, and kept the overflow hole open as we cranked away.

At last the turning got too difficult for us kids and the adults took over. It was almost ready. We bounced around, trying to will it to freeze faster as our mouths watered in anticipation.

At last it was ready to open. The ice and salt were cleared away from the top of the freezer can, and the lid was removed. It looked so delicious, that smooth, white ice cream with the succulent peaches mixed through it. We tingled with excitement.

Dad patiently pulled the dasher out bit by bit, carefully using a spoon to scrape the ice cream that clung to it back into the can. By now we were all salivating at a rate to put Pavlov's dog to shame. Then Dad got some ice cream on his finger and licked it off. He turned his head and spat. It was salty—really salty!

All of us had to taste to see if it was really that bad. It was. We ended up throwing it out to the hogs. Dad said the hogs wouldn't eat it, either. Upon inspection, we found a crack in a seam of the freezer can.

Well, we had our mouths set for ice cream, and we were not going to be deterred by a little setback like this. Mom said she had some sugar saved back for a canning job and some Karo syrup. Aunt Mildred said she had some more sugar too. So we drove back to town and got the syrup, the sugar and more ice.

Meanwhile, Uncle Frannie got out a soldering iron and a blowtorch. The crack was repaired and tested. We sacrificed the last of our precious sugar to make a new batch of ice cream.

Now, I'm sure that it all turned out well and that we enjoyed it immensely. But I have no recollection of how it tasted. All I remember is the anticipation and the crushing disappointment of that first batch. ❖

Shoe Shortage

*By Ann Casper
as told to Jeannie Moore*

During the days of World War II, almost everything was rationed. One such item was shoes. To make mine last, my mother glued the sides together and put cardboard soles in them.

I walked to school with my brothers, over rough ground and under a few fences. One day, school was interrupted by heavy snowfall, and our teacher dismissed us early. The snow soaked my shoes. My feet felt like icicles at first. Then there was little feeling at all.

My brothers walked faster than I could. When I ran to catch up, I fell facedown in the snow. Snow covered my face, my coat and my shoes. I knew that if I didn't hurry, I'd freeze. My loving older brother picked me up and carried me home horseback-style.

When we finally arrived at home, Mom met us at the door. She looked at me and said, "Take your shoes off. Put your feet in this warm water. They will begin to hurt, but keep them in the water anyway."

Mom had tears in her eyes, but she never said anything. I discovered later that she knew my feet had frozen.

When the weather cleared, Mom went to the one country store in the area. She bought me a pair of shoes with the money she had saved for emergencies from the eggs she sold. Mom must have believed that getting new shoes for me was an emergency.

When she handed me the new shoes, black-and-white oxfords, my eyes danced. "Mom, I love them! Thank you!"

Mom smiled and said, "The shoes will see you through, perhaps until the war is over."

Mom was right. I loved my new shoes and took good care of them. I never knew how she got the shoe ration stamps, but somehow she did. ❖

A Tire Tale

By Donna Schmaltz

Remember tire rationing? I'll never forget it! My dad operated a combination service station and one-bay garage during World War II. He had been appointed the tire inspector for our small town. The job of crawling around car undercarriages caked with snow or mud to record tire serial numbers fell to me, a 15-year-old girl.

Cajoling county rationing boards into issuing permits for new tires to our customers was part of the routine. One customer had a pickup he needed for farm hauling. A tire was really necessary, but the rationing board was adamant. "No permit."

"We have the tire available," I persisted. The gentlemen did not relent. I don't remember exactly what each of us said. I do remember that after quite a lot of disagreement, I won my case. The customer got his tire.

New inner tubes were almost impossible to find. Steel-belted radials had not yet been invented, and vehicles had many flat tires due to punctured inner tubes. To salvage them, Dad bought a vulcanizing machine. This contraption fused two pieces of rubber under high heat and pressure. Its heating pad was 3 or 4 inches square; if the area to be repaired was larger, it had to be done a section at a time.

Making these repairs often fell to me. There were three categories of holes: the usual, the remake and the impossible.

The usual was just a nail hole or something similar, and it was a snap to fix. The remake required the customer to furnish an old truck tube. I knew its size and the size of the tire casing it was to be used in.

Calculating with pi, it was possible to cut the excess length off the old tube. Then a collar of cold rubber was fashioned inside one end of the truck tube and the other end was fitted over the collar to meet the first end. After a series of vulcanizing heats, a usable car tube of the correct size was produced. I manufactured such an inner tube many times.

Soon, the entire tire-repair process fell to me. This included jacking up the car, removing the wheel, breaking down the casing with old-fashioned tire irons and muscle power, repairing the leak, reassembling the tire and installing it on the car.

The impossible included tractor tubes. These special tubes were filled with fluid to increase weight and traction. It wasn't considered possible to repair them, and normally they were thrown away if they sustained even the smallest puncture. My crowning achievement was the repair of one of these. The challenge I faced consisted of a rip 41 inches long. It required many heats to close the tear caused by a blowout. I repaired it to the best of my ability, and the farmer was pleased. Fifteen years later, Dad asked the man, "How did that tractor tube come out that Donna fixed?"

"It must have been all right," he replied. "I'm still using it, and it isn't leaking."

When I graduated from high school, I went to work in the office of a J.C. Penney store. However, Dad could not find a mechanic to replace me. All the men were in the service. So I quit my nice, clean job and returned to the vulcanizing machine and grease pit, where I changed oil, took cars apart and learned to weld. But when I attained welding skills equal to those of my dad, he no longer allowed me to handle the torch. Women's lib was far in the future.

My days as a grease monkey ended a year or so later, when I married and had to learn a new trade: that of a homemaker. ❖

There were three categories of holes: the usual, the remake and the impossible.

You Never Know

By Dorothy Francis

*I*n the early 1940s, in our little church in Olathe, Kan., the minister frequently spoke of the Second Coming. One Sunday morning when I was sitting in our hard oak pew, smelling candle wax and hoping the sermon would be short, I thought that the Second Coming had actually happened. A tall man dressed in spotless summer whites decorated with heavy gold braid on the sleeves and shoulders entered our church, walked down the main aisle and seated himself front and center.

Adults looked at him from the corners of their eyes. Kids stared openly, craning their necks, even standing up to peer and whisper. If the man in white noticed this attention, he never let on. Nothing like this had ever happened in our town.

But no, it wasn't the Second Coming. The man was an admiral from the new naval air station that the federal government had just opened a few miles outside our sleepy little village. The Navy had come to town—right in landlocked Kansas. Olathe citizens were wary. *Bolt your doors. Watch your daughters. You never know what those men will do.*

The Navy had come to town—right in landlocked Kansas.

Housing was at a premium for military families who didn't live on the base. I almost burst with excitement when a lieutenant and his family rented the house next to ours. They had two children, and they needed a baby sitter. Me?

Unfortunately, no. Cautious parents didn't allow their daughters to baby-sit for these strangers. In the first place, whoever heard of such a thing as a baby-sitter in those days? If parents wanted to go out, fine, but they took their kids along. No baby-sitting for me. *You never know what those men will do.*

Mother and I took Lt. Comfort and his family a plate of carrot cookies the day they moved in. This was a rare treat because sugar required ration stamps plus money, and we barely had enough sweetener for our breakfast oatmeal.

When we stepped into the Comfort home, packing boxes greeted us standing half-open with their contents scattered about.

From movies I'd seen at our local Dickinson Theater, I knew that the shiny silver container perched on a wooden packing crate was a cocktail shaker. I knew those delicate stemmed glasses were martini glasses. No food or ordinary dishes met our gaze, but Mrs. Comfort smiled and offered us a cocktail. "Dan likes a drink when he gets home from work," she said.

I could hardly believe it. She spoke of this man who taught cadets to fly naval planes just as if he were an ordinary person coming home from an ordinary job. When *my* dad came home from work, all he wanted was his easy chair, John Cameron Swayze reading news on the radio, and the fragrance of supper wafting from the kitchen.

We declined Mrs. Comfort's offer of a martini and made a hasty exit. Cocktail, indeed! Obviously these people from the unlikely sounding place called Hastings-on-Hudson in New York didn't know they were in the Bible Belt.

At school the next day, I could hardly wait to tell the kids of our experience with the Comforts. For a while, I was the center of attention. Then a classmate revealed that her parents were allowing her to baby-sit. I lost the limelight immediately. Evidently, her parents didn't worry about *what those men might do*. All of us girls were pea-green with envy.

My parents raised strawberries in our garden patch. One Sunday when they were ripe, Mom took a heaping box over to the Comfort family. They acted as if they had never seen strawberries fresh from the patch before. I wondered where they got strawberries. Were there no strawberry patches in Hastings-on-Hudson, N.Y.?

"Any special way you fix them?" Lt. Comfort asked, tasting a berry straight from the box. He then shared them with his two children, who soon looked as if they were bleeding from the mouth.

"If we have sugar, we usually sugar them down and add cream," Mother answered. "But if you haven't any sugar, they're delicious straight from the patch."

"We have sugar, but we don't have any cream," Lt. Comfort said.

"I'd lend you some," Mom replied, "but we're out too."

"I'll go get us some," Lt. Comfort said, popping another sweet berry into his mouth.

Mom shook her head. "No grocery stores are open in Kansas on Sunday. It's the law."

Lt. Comfort smiled. "We'll see."

We headed for home as he thanked us, took the strawberries and went inside. A short time later, he and a friend left in his car, and we went on about our Sunday activities.

An hour or so later, Lt. Comfort appeared at our door, carrying a cup of sugar and a pint jar of thick cream. Nobody thought about fat or cholesterol in those days.

"For your strawberries," he said, offering the gifts to my mother. "We can get sugar from the commissary on the base, and I found us some cream."

"Where on earth did you buy cream on a Sunday?" Mom asked as she held the cup of sugar as if it were the crown jewels. I took the jar of cream.

"Got the cream from a farmer," Lt. Comfort said. "Drove to the air base and revved up my trainer plane. Just flew around the countryside until I spotted a pasture filled with cattle. I landed the plane, and a farmer came running out, sort of excited."

"You landed an airplane in his pasture?" Mom's eyes grew wide with surprise. From the tilt of her chin, I could tell that she was squelching laughter.

"Yes. It was a fairly smooth piece of land. No problem at all in landing. The farmer said something about scaring his cows, and I apologized. When I asked for a quart of cream, he just shook his head and didn't say anything.

"By then, his wife had joined us. She invited me to their house. When we were inside, she went to the refrigerator and found some cream for me. I gave her a few dollars, and she seemed real happy about the whole thing."

"I don't believe it!" Mom gasped and began laughing. "A few dollars for cream!"

"I think the farmer's name is Hoff. She wants her canning jars back, so I gave her your name. Hope that was all right."

"That's fine. I know her, and I'll get her jars back to her."

Mom accepted the cream, and we had the best strawberry shortcake with sugar that I've ever tasted.

"You just never know what those men will do," Mom said, still laughing about Lt. Comfort landing his plane in a farmer's pasture.

Later, we did know just what those men would do. They'd win a war for us! Lt. Comfort, if you're still around Hastings-on-Hudson—we're forever grateful! ❖

Stamp Collecting

By Robert F. Snell

D uring World War II, commonly referred to as "the Great War," life in the United States was much different than it is today. Those who were not around then cannot imagine what it was like. Some would not believe they were living in this great country of ours. The U.S. Office of Price Administration issued food-stamp books that were used to purchase goods that were in short supply. The book's front cover cautioned us to not buy rationed goods without the stamps and to never pay more than the legal price. Price ceilings on various items were conspicuously posted on grocery shelves. The motto was "If you don't need it, DON'T BUY IT."

Our government instructed us: "Rationing is a vital part of your country's war effort. Any attempt to violate the rules is an effort to deny someone his share and will create hardship and help the enemy." Meat, canned goods, sugar and coffee were a few of the items that could be purchased only in limited quantities. Tires, gasoline and cigarettes were only available with the appropriate stamps.

New terms entered our vocabulary. One of the most dreaded was *black market*. This meant that people would sell their stamps to others for a premium price, much like scalping tickets to athletic events today. It also meant that retailers would cheat, selling products to customers for cash at higher prices instead of using the stamps as the government required. This practice made many people unhappy and angry. Concerned citizens were disgusted with anyone who would try such tactics.

1942 Staley's waffle syrup ad, courtesy House of White Birches nostalgia archives

Some families traded stamps with other families. One family might swap their coffee stamps for another family's sugar stamps, for instance.

The food shortages taught people to be more patient when grocery shopping. Standing in line for 30 minutes to an hour for a loaf of bread was not uncommon. And if I was one of the lucky ones who got a loaf, it might not even be sliced.

A new form of stamp collecting became popular in 1942. People purchased War Savings Stamps in denominations of 10, 25 and 50 cents and $5. Every Friday, our grade-school class walked to the post office to purchase our stamps, which we pasted in a war-bond stamp book. When filled, it equaled $18.75 and could be used to purchase a Series E savings bond that could be redeemed in 10 years for $25.

Twenty-five million students participated in this part of the war effort, purchasing $25 billion worth of bonds. The purpose of this program was not only to assist our country, but also to teach good citizenship.

The Great War was also the beginning of our recycling programs. We were encouraged to cut the tops and bottoms from tin cans and smash them. The stamp-book slogan read: "Important: When you have used your ration, salvage the TIN CANS and WASTE FATS. They are needed to make munitions for your fighting men. Cooperate with your local Salvage Committee."

War Food Administration poster, House of White Birches nostalgia archives

Once I taped my name and address inside one smashed can. Later I received a letter from a person in Czechoslovakia. A Czechoslovakian friend of my mother's translated it for me. The letter thanked me for helping fight the Axis powers.

We also gathered milkweed pods, which were used to make parachutes. Aluminum foil from gum wrappers was collected, too, as were newspapers, which we tied in bundles.

A friend of mine remembers seeing the gymnasium of an elementary school half-full of newspapers stacked all the way to the ceiling. The papers were used for packing in large munition shells.

Copper pennies weren't to be found because all available copper was used to make shell casings. Pennies then were made from lead, and were a grayish white. You also couldn't find women's nylon hosiery.

The town siren signaled blackouts. At nighttime we had to turn off all our lights for 30–45 minutes, until the blackout was lifted. Curtains and blinds were pulled down; sometimes we even put sheets over windows to prevent any speck of light from showing outside. We reasoned that if enemy aircraft ever attacked, the bombers would not be able to spot the cities and towns below in the dark.

One Christmas the government told us that we could not even turn on our Christmas tree lights! This upset me so much that I wrote to President Truman. But my mother didn't mail the letter, and I still have it.

When servicemen and women came home on leave, they were welcomed with open arms, like celebrities. If there was a parade while they were home, they were always in it, riding in cars with their names on placards on the sides, or walking up front, directly behind the United States flag. These people were our heroes because they were defending our country. And we civilians were heroes to them because of the sacrifices we were making at home to support them overseas.

Children were fascinated by uniforms, especially the insignias sewn on the sleeves. Collecting these became a popular hobby. My collection from all branches of the Armed Forces is still intact.

World War II was a time when we all learned to pull together for the good of our country. We learned to live with shortages and to be tolerant of inconveniences.

Now, as I reflect on those times, I appreciate all the more those men and women who made the ultimate sacrifice so that we could enjoy the good life we have today. ❖

Wartime Rendering

By Rose McAfee

During World War II, I was a young housewife in Cambridge, Ohio. We learned many things in those years, but mostly we learned to do without luxuries and make do with what we had.

We raised gardens and canned the vegetables for winter use. We ate mostly vegetables because meat was rationed. We walked everywhere, saving our rationed gas. We did it all "for the boys" who were fighting for our country overseas.

My husband was in war work at the Cambridge Army Sub-Depot. He also had a pickup truck, and he hauled meat to stores from the local slaughterhouse.

Albert, the owner of the slaughterhouse, asked me if I knew how to render lard. Everyone used lard before vegetable shortening became popular. I didn't know how to render lard, but after receiving a few instructions, I was in business.

I put the strips of hog fat and leaf lard into a large kettle and heated it until the liquid grease melted out. Then I strained the hot, liquid lard through a clean white cloth into a 5-gallon lard bucket. After the straining, all that remained were what we called "cracklings." These edible bits were crisp and brown, like pieces of deep-fried pork. The melted lard cooled and solidified into a beautiful white shortening. The lard sold well for the slaughterhouse owner.

I'll never forget the days I spent rendering lard for the war market. Today, Crisco and other vegetable shortenings are preferred, but lard served us well during the war. ❖

No Stamps, No Sale

By Rosemary Bennett

Raise your hand if you remember ration stamps—if you remember when hen's eggs were as scarce as hen's teeth. The war effort took first dibs on almost everything—from artichokes to zucchini, automobiles to zippers, it was rationed. I was 9 years old when sugar rationing began, and for six years I missed my personal favorites of soda pop, bubble gum and candy bars.

Ration stamps were a kind of currency, and all the money in the world wasn't worth a plugged nickel if you didn't have them. The stamps were color-coded red or blue, dated and given letter names, and they carried point values. The values and exemption dates shifted constantly.

Divine intervention was needed if you lost your ration book or had it stolen. Replacing a lost stamp book required hours of hassling and haggling with the local ration board.

Everyone we knew planted victory gardens. "Meatless Tuesday" was a national slogan, but many other days were also meatless simply because meat was not to be found in any market.

We remember imitation chocolate tasting like paraffin, imitation cheese that tasted like wax, and imitation butter that *was* wax! Do you recall that lardlike white goo—a low-grade, makeshift oleomargarine? It came with a little gold pill. Once the colored pill was worked into the lard stuff, the whole mess turned a bad yellow. We spread it on toast for years. Yuck!

Coffee was recycled. And recycled. The grounds were reused, and by the third or fourth boiling, the coffee was anemic. Is it true that ersatz coffee made from ground-up acorns replaced the real thing on grocery shelves? I can't find anyone to vouch for that rumor.

The county home demonstration agent passed out recipe sheets suggesting food substitutes.

Divine intervention was needed if you lost your ration book or had it stolen.

One recipe was Sugarless, Butterless and Milkless Cake. What were the ingredients? Your guess is as good as mine.

Mom fed us on a ration-stamp shoestring. That sweet old gal could juggle both food and stamps like a circus magician.

Empty shelves at the grocery were the norm. We all got used to it and did without, except those who hoarded, stole or traded on the black market.

Dad was the county agricultural agent; because he traveled the area, he was allowed more gas than most folks. "Essential for the war effort" was the official speakese.

One morning we went to the car to find the gas tank siphoned dry. The tires were also gone, and the car sat on blocks. I hesitate now to tell the family indiscretion that I swore to keep secret so many years ago.

I don't remember how we got there—probably on tires borrowed from a neighbor—but in the dark of night, we drove into a black market House of Tires! Dad bought four "hot" tires and paid through the nose. He might even have bought back his own tires. My parents were not stern or strict, but they clearly informed me that this hot-tire deal was a secret. And they meant it!

Uncle Sam was watching too. From the post office wall, his message seemed to be directed at me: "Loose Lips Sink Ships!"

The threads of painful punishment hung heavy over my head. Authorities. Priorities. Problems! Obey my parents, or Uncle Sam will get me. I worried for weeks lest the secret slip. And then I forgot it. Until now.

So you are the first to hear the hot-tires secret. Nearly 50 years ago, I crossed my heart and hoped to die. Trust me. I can keep a secret—especially when it's forgotten for 50 years.

If Uncle Sam still hangs out at the post office, all us loose lips will be in trouble. ❖

HONOR ROLL

TOWN HALL

ASE GAIR H	DRISCOLL DANIEL B	GREEN HENRY W	KOWALSKY PAUL	NALE JOHN S	RYAN JOHN E
GE RUSSELL	DUFFY CORNELIUS	GISH CARL K	KRONICK THOMAS	NASH LLOYD W	SARNO AUGUST J
SKA ALEX	DUFFY GEORGE E	GUNN COLIN	LANIER BERWICK B	NELSON R.M.	SCHLAET CARL
ESKA STEPHEN	DUFFY JAMES J	GREENBERG NATH	LARSEN WALTER	NOLAN P MARSHALL	SEELEY STANLEY
ISTIE H.B.	DUFFY WALTER	HALL JOHN C JR	LAWSON VICTOR L JR	NORRIS HOWARD	SHUKIE STEVE J
RCH JOHN W	DUKE F DUSOSSOIT	HALL MYRLE	LEAHY JOHN E	NUGENT JAMES R	SKAU FRED
RCHILL ALBERT P	DUNN JOHN S	HALL WALTER N	LEARY ROBERT T	NUZZO DANNY	SKAU CARL
RK WILLIAM P	DUPONT ALBERT E	HARDING CYRIL	LEE ARTHUR K	OBRIEN JOSEPH B	SMITH DOUGLAS
ATES HUDSON	DURNER ARTHUR	HERMENZE JAMES A	LEES WILLARD H	OLSON JARVIS	SMITH IRA
K HOWARD A	DUTCHER BURTIN	HERMENZE SUSAN	LIST THOMAS	ORVIS SCHUYLER A JR	SMITH MILLARD E
PER OTIS	EDWARDS SAMUEL A	HINDS MELVIN R	LITTAURER KENNETH P	PALMER PETER	SMITH STEPHEN
RONE ANTHONY	ELLIS GORDON H	HOLMAN GUY JR	LLOYD EDWARD E	PAYNTER THOMAS G	SOKOLOFF MARTIN N
IG EDOUARD	ELLIS JOHN	HOLLAND VICTOR	LODGE JOHN D	PELL HOWLAND H JR	SOLTES ANTHONY J
TIS ALISON I	FANTON LESTER	HORVATH STEPHEN	LONG ERNEST O	PRATT RODNEY	SOUPPA RALPH A
SEO ANGELO	FEENEY JAMES	HUBBLE G.R.	LOVEJOY JOSEPH JR	PICARD CHARLES	SPENCER J BEAUMONT
SEO FRANCIS	FENTON ROBERT B	HUNT MYRON W	LUCIANO ANTONIO	PLATT JOHN H	STAHURSKY FRANK A
SEO NICHOLAS	FERRIS RODNEY F	INTAS EDWARD R	LUCIANO CHARLES	POWERS GEORGE	STEPHENSON GEORGE
SEO WILLIAM	FESTA THOMAS A	IZZO SALVATORE	LYFORD JOSEPH	POWERS THOMAS	STETSON BASIL W
EO ANGELO J	FIKE JOHN W JR	JANKOSKI JOHN J	LYFORD ROGER	PRATT THOMAS	STETSON CHARLES P
IS REZIN	FLYNN CHARLES	JENNINGS JOHN C	MACKNO JOHN	PRESTON DAVID R	STETSON EUGENE W JR
MARIA JOHN	FOSS CALVIN W	JENNINGS PHILIP S	MADDOCK CURTIS	PURCELL WILLIAM L	STEWART ALEXANDER
MATTIO SABINO	FOX WILLIAM L	JOHNSON PETER	MADDOX GEORGE H	REALE ARTHUR	STODDARD DAVID GOULD
MEO CARMINIA	FRATINO PATSY	KAY JOHN	MALINS VICTOR	RICE ARTHUR H	STRACHAN DONALD C
PUY R ERNEST	FRAZER MARC	KANTOR JOHN L	McCOBB HARRY W	RIPPE ALBERT J	SWEENEY RICHARD A
VEAUX LYLE C	FREEMAN G DAMON	KEENE JOHN H	McGILL W CHARLES	RITTER FRED W	SWEENEY ROBERT
TRICH C PORTER-	FULLER ROBERT E	KELLY GIFFORD	MILLER KENNETH	RITTER GEORGE	SYCH WALTER P
OD ALLEN R JR	GAIR GEORGE JR	KELSEY WESTON M	MEYERS WILLIAM T	RITTER JACK S	JAGATAC ELPIDIO P
AN JOHN	GARTH SHERIDAN H	KELTON JOHN T	MILLS LEWIS	ROGERS ROBERT	TAYLOR GEORGE WALTER
AHER EDWARD	GILBERTIE MOSES	KIRBY WILLIAM C	MOFFETT EDWARD	ROHR ROBERT	THOMPSON ARTHUR C
AHER ROBERT	GORDON RICHARD	KLING JUNE	MONROE PAUL	ROSASCO JAMES	THRUSH DONALD T
TA JAMES T	GRAHAM DAVID	KLING ROBERT	MONROE WILLIAM L	ROY JEAN C	TIERNEY HOWARD S JR
HERTY WILLIAM	GRANT FRANCIS	KOSTER WILLIAM C	MORTON JAMES L	ROY QUENTIN V	TILLINGHAST CHARLES
VAS JOHN J JR	GRAY JOSEPH L	KOVLAK PETER	MUNCE HOWARD	RUBINS JAMES E	TOLLIVER JASON D

TORSKA HENRY F	WILSON DOUGLAS B
TORTORELLA FRANK	WINTON JOHN
TOWNSEND EDWARD H	WORLFORTH ERNEST B
TRACEY JAMES C	WOLF GEORGE W JR
TREMONTE ANTHONY P	WOOD HARRY T
TROY EDWARD B	WOODS RALPH
TROY LOREN	WOODSON ARTHUR R
TROY VINCENT	YOST JOSEPH B
TWARDA JOHN	ZAKOS STEVE JR
TWARDA PETER	
URCIUOLI ROCCO	
VANDERBILT HOOK D	
VANDERBILT ROBERT G	
VANGOR CORNELIUS	
YANI MICHAEL J	
VAN ZANDT JAY C	
VENO NICHOLAS	
VIGILANTE JOSEPH	
WACHOB ROLAND	
WAKEMAN BURRITT M	
WAKEMAN EDWARD	
WAKEMAN ROBERT	
WARD PAUL W	
WARRINGTON BENNIE M	
WASSELL CHARLES P	
WASSELL FRANK L JR	
WASSELL HARRY	
WEBB FRANK E	
WEINGARTNER FRANK	
WELCH HERBERT G	
WELLS SHELDON B	
WENNRICH CARL A	
WENNRICH GEORGE	
WHITE JAMES E	
WILLIAMS DOUGLAS	
WILLIAMS EARL L	
WILLIAMS HERCULES	
WILLIAMS PHILIP HALE	

Stevan Dohanos

The Loss of Innocence

By Doris Hier

When I was little, my world was also small and untouched by the world at large. We didn't have family discussions about national news, or indeed, international events. My knowledge of the outside world came from the newsreels at the Saturday movies that I got to see once in a great while.

When I was 8 years old, the war didn't seem real; it had had very little direct effect on my life. Then my cousin was killed, and so was a boy from our neighborhood. I felt the sadness all around me. The graphic newsreels that showed such destruction became a reality.

My comfortable existence had been threatened. The sounds of planes overhead were no longer just part of normal life. After losing a family member and a friend in the war, I was terrified that we, too, could be bombed whenever a plane went over.

Around town, homes that had family members in the service displayed banners in their windows with blue stars for those serving, a custom that originated back in 1917. When a family suffered the loss of a loved one, a gold star replaced the blue.

There were ration books—one each for my parents, my brother and me (I still have mine). Many items were hard to get. Whenever those rare items arrived in stores, there were long lines of people waiting to purchase them.

Sometimes people waited in lines that wound clear around the corner, only to find that the newly available merchandise was something they didn't use or need. They bought it anyway and sold it to someone farther back in the line.

Every bit of metal went to the war effort. I wanted a bicycle, but they were not available.

> *When I was 8 years old, the war didn't seem real. Then my cousin was killed.*

More affluent people wanted new cars, but they had to put their names on long waiting lists until they were available again. The local newspaper ran a photo of a prominent citizen who got his new car after months of waiting. As he drove it off the lot, another automobile came along and crashed into his brand-new vehicle.

Every block in the neighborhood had an air-raid warden who made sure that all windows were covered and that no lights were visible when there was an drill.

There were also air-raid drills in school, where Friday was "stamp day." I vaguely remember pasting 10-cent stamps into a booklet, which went toward buying bonds for the war effort. Some actually got bonds! I was awed that some kids could actually get $18.75 together to purchase a $25 bond.

When I was 12, the war ended. Families were reunited, except for those who had gold stars in their windows.

Generally speaking, the country had an air of optimism once again. And even through their grief, the gold-star families felt pride that their loved ones had served our country.

The movie *The Best Years of Our Lives* won an Academy Award the following year. It offered an intimate view of how the war had changed the lives of returning GIs.

When the war ended, I was glad that we could turn on the radio and not hear news of battles. I was starting eighth grade, and was already thinking about starting high school. Wow! That would *really* be fun!

One relative brought home an English war bride. My late cousin's wife remarried. Two other cousins went back to school, to finish high school. And life went on. ❖

Facing page: *Honoring the Dead* by Stevan Dohanos © 1943 SEPS: Licensed by Curtis Publishing

We Can Do It!

Chapter Four

The "can-do" spirit of the war years was contagious. When there was a nursing shortage, Nelda Johnson Liebig's Girl Scout troop in Oklahoma City, Okla., rushed in to help fill the void. "World War II Volunteer" was her story published in our magazine in 2003. In it she wrote:

"During World War II, civilians of all ages wanted to do their part in the war effort. I wondered what—if anything—I, a 14-year-old girl, could do for my country. One day my opportunity came when my Girl Scout leader told our troop that we would be enrolling in a nine-week home-nursing course and be certified as official Girl Scout hospital aides.

"We studied the Red Cross nursing manual and learned patient care and bedside manners. We were proud to be accepted as volunteers at St. Anthony Hospital in Oklahoma City.

"Although my family had two cars, they were used only when absolutely necessary, as gas rationing was a way of life. On Saturday mornings I proudly donned my forest green hospital uniform and walked two miles to the city bus line, which terminated at the corner of Southeast 29th and Easter Avenue. I paid my fare—two tokens for a quarter—and rode 20 blocks, then transferred to the downtown bus. On Main Street I had my third and last transfer to the hospital, which was in the northern section of the city. My workday began at 9:30 a.m.

"Like most hospitals during the war, St. Anthony functioned with a skeleton staff. Many of the former medical staff had joined the military or had been drafted. In the face of such personnel shortages, some retired nurses returned to work.

> *I wondered what—if anything—*
> *I could do for my country.*

"Seven members of my troop were assigned to floor duty. We did virtually everything that registered nurses did except administer drugs. I was assigned to work in the sterilizing room. Every item possible was cleaned, repaired, sterilized and pressed into service over and over. Recycled surgical gloves were cleaned, patched and sterilized to be used anywhere except in surgery.

"Our troop leader, Emily McCord, told us we would receive a patch for our uniforms after 90 hours of service. However, I lost count after 300 hours. The national Scouting office asked if we were willing to have the thread and dye for the proposed patches go to the war effort instead. We were indeed.

"At the end of the war in 1945, my brother, Charles, was honorably discharged from the U.S. Marine Corps. Mom returned to her life as a busy farm wife and mother. Dad developed his own business as an independent oil producer. Martha married her sailor boy stationed at the Norman Air Naval Station when he returned home from the South Pacific. I retired my green pinafore, which by now was faded and stained.

"Not only had I contributed to the war effort, but I knew I wanted to continue to be active in the Girl Scouts of America. And I was, for 25 years. And it all began with my desire to become a volunteer and do my part for my country in 1944."

Nelda's words remind me of one of my father's favorite sayings. If I was discouraged and ready to quit trying to do any particular task, he always said, "'Can't' can't do anything!" That taught me the same attitude that Nelda learned: "We can do it!"

—Ken Tate

My Mom Was a "Rosie"

By Kathy Manney

When I was growing up in the 1940s, "Rosie the Riveter" was my measure of women's liberation, long before the women's rights movement of the 1970s. Mom, Aunt Mildred and my grandmother typified Rosie, whose endearing wartime image and can-do spirit have become an American icon. During World War II, while embracing jobs that were sometimes dangerous, my mom, and other women who worked outside the home, played a leading role in supporting combat troops overseas. These women were the army on the home front.

Nowadays, few remember that before World War II, frozen food was not generally available. There was no Pentagon, no penicillin, no baby boom—and before World War II, no one had ever heard of Rosie the Riveter. Talking about those days, Mom said, "There was a camaraderie because we were all working for the same cause. So many of us were in the same boat, literally, and we had a common goal: to help win that war."

Mom helped build 50 "baby flat-top aircraft carriers" as well as other ships.

I grew up in Portland, Ore. I remember when the Portland-Vancouver area was home to three shipyards where production crews worked around the clock. Mom helped build 50 "baby flat-top aircraft carriers" as well as many other ships.

With her husband serving in the Pacific Theater and with a young child to support, Mom began her shipbuilding career at the Vancouver Kaiser Shipyard for the Buckler Co., a subcontractor on the Columbia River.

Her wartime "uniform" consisted of sturdy shoes, coveralls, a hard hat and a bandanna tied around her head.

Mom began as a taper. Tapers cut and pasted strips of tape over the seams in the fiberglass insulation that was welded to the bulkheads to prevent fiberglass from seeping out. Women made good tapers because it was very methodical detail work, much like wallpapering.

Tapers followed the electricians, and Mom's hands were often scratched and cut by electric cable, leaving lifelong scars. She said it was common for tapers to have to visit the first-aid office to have fiberglass washed out of their eyes. The tapers also worked near the workers who covered the pipes and air ducts with asbestos. Fortunately, Mom has never had any sign of ingesting asbestos.

Despite these hazards, occupational safety was not an issue in the 1940s. Shipyard workers did not have earplugs to shut out the noise or safety glasses to protect their eyes.

Mom was the youngest and slimmest on her team, so her crew leader often assigned her to jobs in the tightest places of the ship. Once while she was lying on top of an air duct, with about 6 inches between her and the bulkhead she was working on, the pipe fitters began testing the pipes without checking to see if the area was clear. The room immediately filled with steam from a leaky pipe. Only by quickly half-falling and half-jumping from her perch did Mom escape serious burns.

Lunchtime at the shipyard lasted an all-too-brief 30 minutes. During this break, the tapers had to wash their hands in mineral spirits to remove the sticky glue. By the time they left the ship to go to the restroom, get their pail and find a place to eat, there was little time to actually eat.

Rosies like Mom helped win the war. Wartime shipyard workers could produce a cargo ship in 17 days. When it came to wartime materials, they simply out-produced all other countries.

Recently, while searching through some papers about those years, I came across this toast that Joseph Stalin had made to President Franklin Roosevelt: "To American

The work of women was indispensable to the war effort in the 1940s. Above: A worker in a war production plant adjusts a machine part. Photo courtesy House of White Birches nostalgia archives. Left: The author and her mother. Note the slacks. During these years, women's fashions would be changed forever. Below: The "2" on the author's mother's workplace badge signifies second shift. Note that this round identification button is very similar to the one on the woman in the poster on the facing page. The Women's Ordnance Worker poster was produced for the U.S. Army by Adolph Treidler in 1943.

production, without which this war would have been lost."

But the Allied victory didn't alleviate the rigorous demands on shipyard workers. V-E Day was a signal for production to swing all of its might and resources in support of our forces in the Pacific, bringing a speedier end to the war against Japan.

When her job at the Vancouver yard was completed in March 1945, Mom and some of her co-workers went to the Oregon Shipyard on Swan Island in the Willamette River in Portland. Here she truly became a Rosie the Riveter, riveting pontoons destined for dry docks in the South Pacific.

It wasn't long before Mom was promoted to layout. Her surroundings were as noisy as before, but the work was easier, as she read blueprints and marked where the riveting was to be done.

In August 1945, on the very day Mom and I moved into a new home, Mom reported to work as usual. But she and her co-workers were told to go home; the first atomic bomb had been dropped on Japan.

Mom's war effort was over. The pontoons were not going to be finished. So ended my mother's ship-building career.

My mom, Rosie the Riveter and other women like her were feminist pioneers. They knew about strength, independence, solidarity and social issues that seem current to women today. Some might think, for instance, that the issue of child day care is relatively new. During the war years, day care was often subsidized by the government, and frequently was provided on site by defense employers, including Kaiser.

Mom found a warm and loving elderly family to care for me during those years. I lived in their home during my mother's working days and came home during her days off. Though I was very young, I can remember telling people, "My mommy works in the shippy-yard, and my daddy is in the Pill-a-peens."

In the Good Old Days of the 1940s, Mom never heard of "having it all." She simply accepted the need to balance job and family, both for financial reasons and to support our country's demand for defense workers. ❖

"My girl's a WOW"

WOMAN ORDNANCE WORKER

Heroes in Residence

By Harry Bingham

*I*n 1940, war was raging in Europe, and the war clouds were drifting westward at an alarming rate. As one of its defensive measures, the U.S. government constructed an extensive new airport in the heart of southern New Jersey. The installation replaced nearly 1,000 acres of scrub oak and pine trees on a sandy plain.

The new airport was dedicated in August 1941, but its importance wasn't fully realized until the attack on Pearl Harbor and the United States' formal entrance into World War II a few months later. The Millville Air Base, as it then became known, was designated an advanced gunnery base for the stout P-47 Thunderbolt fighter aircraft. This plane was to become a favored armed escort for the bombers that knocked out the industrial centers in Hitler's Germany.

When the day came for Frank to leave town, I realized that I had really bonded with him.

As the base reached its full potential, there was a growing military presence in and around my hometown of Millville, N.J., the home of "America's First Defense Airport" (a moniker proudly given by Millville's local newspaper).

Many young married couples descended on the town looking for rooms, apartments and house-sharing arrangements. They knew that this was likely the serviceman's final training before an overseas assignment, and they wanted to spend their last weeks together.

My mother decided that our family could spare a bedroom, and she opened our home to several such couples during the war. My older sister had just graduated from college and was away teaching, so her bedroom was available. In 1941, my older brother was 15, I was 13 and our kid brother was 6. Our father had died in 1936 of complications from the flu, so you can imagine the potential for hero worship when uniformed airmen came to live with us.

My interest in aviation and things military became secondary to some of the other subjects that our new family members exposed us to. I have especially fond memories of newlyweds Lt. Frank Emory and his wife, Marge. Frank was from Washington state, and Marge was from Virginia. I loved to hear Frank's stories of living, camping and hunting in big mountain country—quite a contrast to the flat country that was my home. And Marge was the first "Southern belle" I had ever met. We all teased her about her Southern drawl and enjoyed showing her around town on afternoon bicycle rides. I suppose I might even have had a secret crush on her.

Facing page: P-47 photograph courtesy of Janice Tate

Just before Frank shipped out to take his place as a P-47 combat pilot in Europe, he got me started on a correspondence course in taxidermy. I have never forgotten the first specimen I tried to stuff. Frank suggested that I begin by mounting a pigeon, but he left town before I completed it. I struggled with it and couldn't get the head quite right. I didn't want to have to write Frank and tell him I had failed in my first attempt as a taxidermist, so I cut off the head and mounted the headless body. Such as it was, it was an early lesson in perseverance and decision making!

When the day came for Frank to leave town, I realized that I had really bonded with him. Watching him wave goodbye from the cockpit as he rolled down the runway on that final morning was an emotional moment for me.

We stayed in touch through occasional correspondence. My favorite letter was one Frank wrote from England on March 27, 1944:

"Harry, I'd like to dedicate a few lines to you and your buddies. ... I really mean every word of this. I know that you guys admire and probably secretly envy us. ... From the standpoint of people at home, we all seem like heroes. ... In reality we are the same kids that lived on your street. ... We get just as scared as you would be, we think the same thoughts you would think, and we don't hate German pilots because we don't know them. We shoot them down because we don't like their airplanes and what they stand for. ... I shot down a FW-190 on the Hanover-Brunswick raid of February 10, and later in the month, probably destroyed two more 190s on the ground at an assembly plant in the Ruhr Valley. Our C.O., Maj. Walter Beckham, was shot down by flak that day, as were two others from our squadron."

In 2001, I reviewed the microfilm for the *New York Times* of Feb. 11, 1944, the day after the Hanover-Brunswick raid. The front-page headlines read:

"ALLIES STAND OFF FOE NEAR ROME AS ATTACKS ON BEACHHEAD MOUNT; U.S. AIR FLEET BATTLES OVER REICH
"84 Planes Bagged"
Here are some excerpts from the text:

"American heavy bombers struck deep into Germany again today. … Mustangs, Thunderbolts and Lightnings that escorted the Flying Fortresses in their attack on Brunswick, and Thunderbolts that operated with three Liberator formations against the airfields in the Netherlands accounted for 55 of the enemy aircraft destroyed. … The cost to the American Air Force of today's operations was 29 bombers and eight fighters."

I guess the main reason for writing this now is to let Frank and Marge and all the others who have touched my life in their special ways know that they were truly my "heroes in residence." Their examples of patriotism and citizenship were not lost on the next generation following on the heels of "The Greatest Generation" (as Tom Brokaw aptly titled his book on World War II).

I completed my engineering degree and ROTC summer camp just one month after the Korean War started. When given the opportunity to choose between the reserves and a regular commission, I opted to go into the Regular Army Corps of Engineers. I served 19 months in Korea, landing less than three months after the war began on June 25, 1950.

During my career in the Army—and many times afterward—I have thought of the young servicemen and their wives who became part of my family for a short time during World War II. They helped to shape my formative years, and I am grateful for the memories. ❖

The author (right) and his friend Herb "Hob" Adams in front of their scoutmaster's home in the early 1940s, about the time of this story.

One Day in History

By Billie B. Chesney

On Aug. 6, 1945, I was about to leave my shift at the switchboard when my supervisor "plugged in" on my board to say that I would be needed to stay overtime. In her excitement, my normally by-the-book Bell Telephone Co. supervisor forgot proper phraseology and blurted, "We're bombing the h--- out of Japan! I need all the help I can get tonight!"

Assuming that her position of authority precluded any argument from me, she moved on down the line, repeating her message to the other long-distance operators.

Thus began one of the longest nights of my life. We had noticed an increase in traffic for some time, and now the boards lit up like a Christmas tree.

The pay-phone trunk lines from nearby Fort Leavenworth blinked constantly. As soon as the ticket on a call was stamped completed, the light came on again. Circuits stayed busy for hours, and far into the night the same phrases were repeated: "There will be a one- (or two-, or three-) hour delay." "We will notify you when we are able to complete your call to Denver (or Seattle, or Memphis)." "Sergeant (Private, Captain), ready on your call to home."

In those days, a call from Leavenworth, Kan., to Small Town, Any State, was routed through Kansas City, Omaha, Atlanta, Oklahoma City and any number of smaller tributaries before making contact. A busy signal or disconnect at any of those relays meant a delay—or the whole process might have to be started all over again.

One particular call stands out in my memory, even after all these years. Placed to a small town in Georgia, it had met with a few of those frustrating delays.

When I finally made the connection, the soldier took a moment to thank me for not giving up before he deposited his money. I'll never forget that. It was about 3 a.m., but he didn't complain about waiting for hours to talk to his wife. He thanked me for not giving up.

When I monitored the call in advance of the warning that their first three minutes were up, they were both crying. I didn't have the heart to interrupt. I stamped the call completed. They talked for maybe 45 minutes. If ever there was a time and reason to break a rule or two, that was the night.

I didn't know until later that we had "bombed the h--- out of Japan" with something called an atomic bomb. As incredible as it seems, I doubt it impressed me much at that time. I was 17, and it seemed we had been at war most of my life. My favorite cousin had been shipped home in a box. Whatever it took to bring the rest of the fathers home in one piece was fine with me.

And maybe that young soldier got back home to Georgia a little sooner. ❖

1944 Bell Telephone ad, courtesy House of White Birches nostalgia archives

I Was a TWERP

By Frances M. Ramsay

*I*t was 1944. My husband was in the Navy aboard ship somewhere in the Pacific. I needed a job, and Mother, who was a Civil Service employee in the post office then, told me that the post office was hiring TWERPs. This was post-office language for a "Temporary Woman Employee Replacing a Permanent," and that's exactly what they meant. Each time a permanent employee was drafted or joined the service, he would be replaced by a temporary worker. It worked in reverse, too, because each time a permanent employee returned to civilian life, a temporary employee was immediately terminated.

Working in the post office was hard work, but fun. I worked with incoming mail; it was then called "city scheme." There were no ZIP codes then and no computers to sort the mail; there were just zone numbers. We had to memorize all the city streets and the division lines for each zone.

> *This was post-office language for a "Temporary Woman Employee Replacing a Permanent."*

To prepare for the employment test, we were given a stack of small cards with city addresses—1,200 cards and a small case divided into numbered pigeonholes. But you didn't look at the numbers—you memorized them. To pass the test, you had to sort 60 cards per minute correctly, and to make sure you still remembered, you repeated the test each year. I got 100 percent each time. I think I was too scared to make a mistake.

I worked the night shift, 5:30 p.m.–2 a.m., six nights and the seventh night off. Sometimes a train was late getting in with the mail, and we'd have to wait. We had to punch out on the time clock and wait in the swing room. I don't know why it was called that. It was sort of a lounge. Sometimes we would "swing" for three or four hours before the train arrived. We wrote letters, read a book, knitted or whatever to occupy our time.

When the mail arrived, our eight-hour shift started. The pay was 75 cents an hour before 6 p.m. and 15 cents an hour more after 6 p.m., so most of my pay was the big rate of 90 cents per hour. If we worked overtime, there was no time-and-a-half rate. It was still 90 cents per hour. I usually earned $45 or $50 a week, and that was really good pay then.

We sat on high stools. A long row of girls and women, about 20 or 25 of us, sat and sorted. It became so automatic that we could even visit and sort mail at the same time, while we kept up with our required speed of 60 pieces per minute. One girl whose husband was in the Army had quite a routine. She would repeat his name each time she tossed a letter into a pigeonhole: "Chuck, Chuck, Chuck." I can hear her yet.

Inspectors were constantly watching from catwalks that ran along the upper walls throughout the entire building. They even went through the ladies' room. There was no idling in there, and absolutely no way anyone could even *think* of being dishonest. You couldn't hide a letter if you had wanted to.

Even though we read only the addresses and not the names as we worked, sometimes your own address or the address of a friend would jump out at you, and if by some chance you came across a letter for yourself from your husband or boyfriend—wow!

You could not, of course, even *think* of waiting till the next day's mail delivery to read that letter. We had a wonderful supervisor. Tom just understood, so when that happened, we took the letter to Tom. He marked it "OK," and we could take a break and go to the swing room to read it.

The only letters we didn't like to sort were the V-mail. Many younger people may not remember V-mail, but lots of us do. Overseas, they simply took pictures of the original letters the servicemen wrote and put it all on microfilm. The letters ended up in very small envelopes about the size of party invitations or birth announcements. The writing was very small, and they were hard to read and hard to hold on to. When we saw the loaders coming with an armload of V-mail, it was funny how so many girls disappeared on a coffee break all at once—anything to get away from the desks.

Sometimes the outgoing mail section would be short of help, and that was another time we'd all hide. Boy! How the city-side girls hated to work the outgoing mail! People today who sort the mail with a computer wouldn't believe what it was like in the 1940s. There was a long narrow table, maybe 10 or 12 feet long, with two slots running along the front of each side. We dropped the short letters down the front slot and the long letters down the back slot. We tossed the thick envelopes and small packages onto a shelf overhead.

The pickup men who gathered mail from the mailboxes all over town kept coming and dumping another sack full on the table. We stood there, people lined up on both sides of the table, and dropped letters in those slots, stamps all headed the right way. It seemed so monotonous.

It's no wonder that when we saw the foreman from the outgoing section coming our way, there was a sudden rush for the ladies' room or the swing room. It didn't always work, though, and we quite often ended up working a three- or four-hour shift at the facing table.

The post office was about two blocks from the train depot, and many times when we went for our dinner at about 10 p.m., the drugstore dining room would be crowded with soldiers and sailors who were killing time between trains. This was a really large drugstore, and it had a big restaurant in the back where we ate each evening.

One evening when my friends Blanche and Judy and I went for dinner, three sailors came over to our booth. One of the fellows appeared older than the others. He might have been about 35 or so, and he did the talking for all of them. He said that they were on their way to San Francisco to ship out. They were lonely and would like to sit with us and visit if we didn't mind.

Well, we looked at one another, trying to decide. Two of us were married girls and the other was engaged, and we never cheated on our fellows, but we agreed it would be OK, so they all crowded into our booth, and immediately each of them showed us pictures of his own wife or girlfriend. The older fellow even showed us pictures of his children.

When it was time for them to return to the depot, they asked if we could come and wave as they boarded the train. We said that we couldn't, as it would make us late to work, so they left.

When we three got back to the post office, I don't know who thought of it first, but we suddenly all were ashamed of ourselves for not going with them. We hurried to the depot as fast as we could, but the train had already left. We were a sad group. It would not have hurt us to be late one time, and it would have made those boys happy to see us wave goodbye.

I worked in the post office for about three years. I eventually changed from the night shift to the day shift. The war had ended, and almost every day, a regular employee would return to work and a TWERP would be dismissed. One day it was me. However, my husband was home by then, as he had been discharged from the Navy a couple of months earlier. ❖

Leaving the Nest

By June Pomerinke

*I*t was 1941. Friends I'd grown up with were being shipped away to distant places. People put their lives on hold to take jobs in defense plants in other parts of the country. My neighbor, who had two sons in the service, wanted to contribute, so when Civil Service examinations were offered for training in service-related areas, Mrs. Tarola and I decided to take them. Shortly thereafter, we had to leave for training.

We only had three months to master the intricacies of tachometers, altimeters, pressure gauges, climb indicators, and turn-and-bank indicators, so we put in full days at school.

Our checks barely covered necessities, but on occasion, a group of us would pool our change for a few games of bowling or a movie.

In December, we were to indicate our choice of depots to transfer to for our employment. I chose Spokane, Wash., which was closest to my home. I got a room at the old Darby Hotel where some of my co-workers were staying. A lone lightbulb hung from the ceiling. Everyone was forbidden to have electric appliances because the hotel was not wired

The SPAD News brought news to the Spokane (Wash.) Army Air Depot workers.
Illustration from the February 1943 SPAD News.

for them, but almost all of us had a single-burner hotplate on which to heat a can of soup.

With the usual government efficiency, when we arrived at the depot, eager to use our new skills, we were advised we would not be repairing the instruments we had studied. Instead we would be working with the gyros from the automatic pilots.

Seeing our dismay, the instructor said, "I don't know anything about them, either! We'll learn together." We were told that this instrument was new and secret, and we were not supposed to talk about it. A few days later, we saw a cutaway of an automatic pilot in a window of the shops, so we concluded it couldn't be too much of a secret.

That winter our class put on a couple of dances. We had a great time at the first dance, but the second was not so successful. The phonograph arrived with only one record—*Give Me One Dozen Roses*. There was a piano at hand, but only one pianist, and he only knew one song—a jazzed-up version of *Melody in F*.

One evening, my sister Nadean and I decided it would be fun to see how many sailors we could pick up in a specified period of time. My friend Mike wasn't enthused about this, but he and my brother Victor followed at a discreet distance to verify our count. There were sailors on every corner and in every doorway. A sideways glance, a shy smile and they fell in beside us. When, after a few blocks, we already had 14 in tow, Mike took his leave.

Pictured are (left to right) a girl from mechanics class, the author and Mrs. Tarola. Ladies were required to wear white blouses and dark blue pants, and cover their hair beneath a white cap. The men wore white coveralls.

Working with gyros was tedious and frustrating. When the repairs were completed, after much lapping of pivots and polishing of races, the inspector would give it the final calibration check, put the wax seal on it, and it was ready to be put back into service. Occasionally we got an instrument that would not check out, so we would tear it down and start over.

Our desks were cramped together, so we were well aware when someone had a problem instrument. That's why it was puzzling when suddenly this instrument was receiving the wax seal from the inspector when we were sure it was not ready to go.

It was general knowledge that the inspector was an alcoholic, but when it leaked out that he was putting his stamp of approval on faulty instruments in exchange for overnight visits from some of the girls, my stomach turned. Men's lives depended on these instruments.

I was not happy in this work, but *this* made it unacceptable. I was warned my resignation would not be accepted during wartime, but when I revealed my reasons, there were no further objections.

My first year away from home culminated in my marriage to Mike, whose health had barred him from service. Our union was no surprise to most, however. When Mike was courting me, my room at the Darby, to quote a friend, "looked like a funeral parlor," as he kept it filled with an endless variety of flowers. ❖

Praise the Lord and Pass the Ammunition

By Joyce Bennett

When I heard that the Japanese had bombed Pearl Harbor, I was working as a hired girl in the druggist's home. Music played softly on the radio as I scrubbed the floor. Suddenly the broadcast was interrupted by the announcer shouting, "Pearl Harbor has been bombed, many have been killed, ships in the harbor were destroyed, planes on the base also!" Soon American planes were in the air, and some Japanese planes were shot down.

That evening, after attending a dance, we young folks gathered in a soda-fountain shop and discussed what to do. Many boys were leaving that next week to enlist in the Army or Navy. Some of the girls, too, would enlist in the Women's Army Corps in Des Moines, Iowa. My sister called me to come to Des Moines. She said we could get on at the large ammunition plant in nearby Ankeny, Iowa, where .50-caliber shells were loaded.

We averaged 10,000–14,000 shells a day.

My sister was employed almost right away. I had my physical and test, but I wouldn't be called to work until the third large building was completed. In the meantime, I worked as an usher at a theater, and later at a business that processed fresh eggs into dried eggs for the boys overseas. When I finally got my call, I was happy, as wages would be higher there—65 cents an hour compared to 35 cents and 50 cents at my other jobs.

There were only five of us starting in the new powder wing where the shells were loaded. Two of us were chosen to be supervisors, and our wages were raised to 69 cents an hour. Many older girls resented this at first since I was only 20 and Rosie was 22.

We estimated that we trained about 200 girls each. We monitored the safety procedures, as we had to wear white overalls, dust caps that completely covered our hair, safety glasses and unattractive safety shoes. But we were glad we were wearing those ugly safety shoes when a heavy die dropped on our toes. The bronze die was about the size of a pint jar and weighed at least a pound.

At the end of the day, we had to tally up the totals of shells loaded off the 10 machines. We averaged 10,000–14,000 shells a day. This was quite a staggering total since we had no calculator or adding machine.

There were 10 rooms in the powder room and four girls and one older man. He worked behind a glass shield, watching carefully as each spoon of powder was put in the shell, one at a time. Sometimes one went off. The explosion caused quite a bang, as all the powder caught fire and burned.

The girls had different stations, adding the shells to each die and keeping them upright. At the final station, a plunger pushed the filled shell out into the waiting cart.

All this was done quickly and efficiently on conveyor belts. To pass the time, we sang war songs. Our favorite was *Praise the Lord and Pass the Ammunition*.

We were proud when our loved ones wrote home that they had used D.M.-imprinted .50-calibers, as my husband did on the B-24 bomber called "Male Call," on which he was the nose gunner. That bomber flew 22 missions over Germany. My two brothers and several cousins used the shells in the infantry in France and other places.

In our window, we placed a small flag with three stars on it—one each for my husband and two brothers. We also placed an ice sign in our window when we needed ice for our icebox. We had no refrigerator.

Many things were rationed: gasoline, rubber tires and other rubber items, denim cloth, sugar, coffee, metal cookware, detergents and other soaps and nylons. We girls painted our legs with a beige cream to resemble nylons; that was fun. But when our panties and bras came without elastic, it *wasn't* fun, and in fact, it was very uncomfortable!

One day I went to every store in Des Moines, looking for a dishpan. Finally I found an enameled oval one. The clerk had put it in the back because of a bad dent, but I was

happy to buy it. I later used it as a bathtub for all three of my children.

Later, visiting my hometown and surrounding farms, there didn't seem to be so many shortages. True, farmers had to ration their gas for the field work, but the housewives said they could always get their soaps and detergents, and

Left: The author and her husband, Jim, during a happy furlough in 1943.
Right: The author was chosen Queen of the War Plant. This was a pinup picture for her husband.

denim jeans and overalls. I guess the smaller stores had anticipated the demand and had had the foresight to stock up.

Looking back, the most difficult part of my wartime job was changing shifts every seven weeks. The shifts ran from 8 a.m.–4 p.m., from 4 p.m.–midnight and from midnight–8 a.m. When we changed shifts, we had to work a day shift after the midnight one, and 16 hours at work was exhausting.

The long hours and changing mealtimes caught up with me, and I had to have an appendectomy. After working at the ammunition plant for three years, I had to quit in 1944.

By then, the war was beginning to subside. By 1945, many other employees had been laid off. Only a skeleton crew of 1,900 remained at the plant that, at its peak in 1943, had employed 20,000. ❖

Pedal Power for Peace

By Barbara Davis

Grandmom's shiny black Singer sewing machine marched off to war in 1942. After years of making baby clothes, party dresses and living-room drapes, the faithful old Singer treadle sewing machine was recruited for the war effort— along with Grandmom.

Hoping to do something useful for the men in the military, a group of neighborhood ladies in Philadelphia formed a sewing circle and volunteered a couple of days every week, working for the American Red Cross. These skillful seamstresses invaded a corner of the basement in the Henry W. Lawton Elementary School, where they set up camp and proceeded to pedal for peace. Grandmom's Singer was loaded onto my wagon and pulled up the street to join the rest of the "troops" for the duration of the war.

One of Grandmom's biggest projects was sewing slippers for the wounded recuperating in military hospitals. She used a pattern to cut the sole and top portion of the slipper, and one size fit all! I can still feel the fabric she used: a bit like velvet, but much more durable. There were only two color choices—maroon and blue-gray. One day, she brought some of the scraps home for me, and I made wall-to-wall carpeting for my dollhouse. Nothing was ever wasted during the war.

While Grandmom was busy sewing for the American Red Cross, my father was away someplace with the Army. Mother got a job in a defense plant, and Grandpop volunteered as an air-raid warden. Mother and I were the only ones who didn't get to wear a uniform, and I was unhappy about that.

However, I found a special duty to perform. It was my job to wash out the empty tin cans after dinner, place the top and bottom tin circles together inside the can, and then jump on it with all of my 40 pounds. Once the cans were flattened, I carried them up the street to the big red, white and blue 55-gallon drum on the corner, where I dumped them for the weekly scrap-metal collection.

Back at the schoolhouse, it seemed like a million pairs of slippers had been made by those Red Cross volunteers and volunteers all over the world. I could just imagine the wounded soldiers

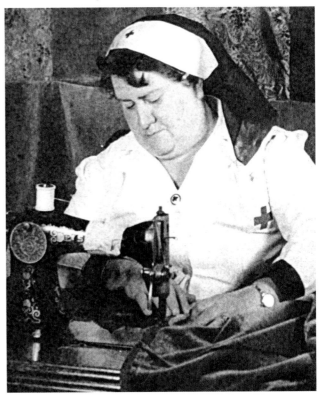

The author's grandmother, Charlotte Shoemaker, Red Cross volunteer, Philadelphia, Pa., 1942–1945.

shuffling around in Grandmom's slippers. The pedal power of those neighborhood ladies in the basement of the school during the hard years of World War II earned them a special citation from the British ambassador. Grandmom was very proud.

When the boys came marching home at the end of the war, the once-shiny Singer was retired with honor and was replaced in Grandmom's sewing room by a brand-new electric model—and yes, it was another Singer. ❖

The Elevator Girl

By Louise T. Heck
as told to John J. Lesjack

*L*iberty High School, class of 1942, was behind me, except for the laughs. I always enjoyed a good laugh. My favorite high school memory was the time I was in archery class with my bow and arrow. I shot an arrow, and not only missed the target, but sent my arrow through the glass door to the school. Luckily, no one was injured.

After graduation, I worked for two years as a clerk for Bethlehem Steel Corp. in their freshly renovated, 13-story headquarters on Third Street in South Bethlehem, Pa. Then, a new position opened up, as young women were selected to be "elevator girls." I recommended a friend of mine for the job, and then she recommended me, but to tell the truth, I was afraid of heights.

The new, state-of-the-art elevators with push-button controls had no gates, but they still scared me. During my interview, I was shown how to operate the car, was allowed to take it up and down a few floors, and I was made to feel safe. I also learned that the job had many perks.

Being an elevator girl was a prestigious job that paid over $100 a week.

Operators would get 30 minutes on and 30 minutes off. They would be issued pretty winter and summer outfits. When I learned the uniforms would be designed exclusively for BSC and would be tailor-made by the CEO Eugene Grace's personal tailor, I was very close to a decision. I was told the girls had to look good because they would give the first impression to businesspeople who visited BSC.

I lived with my parents, Harry and Marguerite Tremaine, and my older brother, Bob. I told them how there would be only six of us who would meet and greet businesspeople, escort them to offices and make introductions. My parents were most impressed that department heads had been notified that the company would not tolerate any unwanted invasion of a girl's personal space, and they encouraged me to accept the position.

Being an elevator girl was a prestigious job that paid over $100 a week, which was good money in those days. A stenographer's starting salary was $23.75 a week. Working in the lobby was more fun than working in an office. I remember how we would watch for the old man from the cleaners to deliver our uniforms. When we saw him come in, we would run over and kiss him just to watch his embarrassment. Then we'd laughingly run back to our cars. Oh, we were so naughty!

In the morning, we had to be ready for CEO Eugene Grace's arrival. We had someone on the roof with binoculars. When Mr. Grace's limo and police escort were spotted, we held an elevator car for him so that he could go directly to his sixth-floor office. I think he rode in my car only once.

The attack on Pearl Harbor caused changes in every one's lives. My brother Bob joined the Navy. Security was tightened at BSC. Gone were the days when a friend would put her foot in the elevator door in the lobby and stick you between floors in an empty car just for laughs. We had also stopped kissing the deliveryman.

I was married during the war, but I was alone at my wedding reception for a very good reason. George Heck, my groom, was in the hospital. He had come home from boot camp by train the morning of the wedding on a seven-day leave. As we came out of the church, people threw rice at us, and some of it lodged in George's ear. It was so painful that he was taken to the emergency room. By the time he got to the reception, the portrait photographer and most people had left. We soon drove off on our honeymoon in the Poconos.

After the war, my husband used his GI Bill to complete work on his engineering degree at Lehigh University. I was allowed to work as an elevator girl until my boss learned I was pregnant. I briefly worked at another job, and then I stayed home with the love of my life, my only daughter, Pamela.

I had received a lot of attention from guests who rode in my car, and I met a lot of interesting people on the job. As an elevator girl, I met many friends. But more importantly, that was where I learned self-confidence and developed an attitude that allowed me to enjoy life wherever I was.

That job has stayed with me all of my life, and here I am, after 85 years of living, still talking about my Good Old Days with the Bethlehem Steel Corp. ❖

Above: The author's engagement photo was taken shortly before she was hired as an elevator girl. You can see why she was selected! Below: The author's wedding. She didn't know until the morning of the wedding whether her fiancé would be there. Sometimes military leaves were rescinded.

Don't Sit Under the Apple Tree

Chapter Five

Many wartime romances flourished in the early 1940s. "Don't sit under the apple tree with anyone else but me," the popular song of the day went. Love hastened many weddings before young men left for boot camp, while some were postponed for the duration of the war. Then there were those, like Sylvia Johnson, whose prince came to her home riding his gallant steed. He was on leave in 1944, and he couldn't wait any longer to make his vows:

"Amos and I planned to be married, but no date was set. He was serving in the Army during World War II, and even though we wrote to each other every day, the mail was censored, so he couldn't tell me when he would be coming home.

"On the morning of April 8, 1944, I was helping my mother cook breakfast when I looked out the front window to see my handsome soldier riding into the front yard on his horse. I was overjoyed to see him, and after a quick touch-up to my hair, I ran out to greet him.

"My father was talking with him as I ran from the house. In those days, it wasn't appropriate to show affection in public—especially in front of your parents—but as Amos stepped down from his horse, there was no way I could keep from kissing him, right in front of my dad!

"Amos would be home for only a few days. We wanted to get married, so we decided that that very day would be just fine. He asked my dad for permission, and with Dad's reluctant consent to give away his youngest daughter, our

There was no fancy wedding dress or tuxedo, and no flowers or music.

plans were in motion. After a visit to the doctor, for blood tests and physicals, and a quick stop at the courthouse, we were off to be married.

"My brother, Raymond, drove us into town in his Model A Ford. He also witnessed the ceremony, which was performed in the front of a store owned by the preacher and his wife. There was no fancy wedding dress or tuxedo, and no flowers or music, but it was a beautiful wedding. I thought I was surely the luckiest woman alive.

"As we left the preacher's home, we met my best friend, Geneva, and her new husband. We all had a big laugh when we found out that they had just gotten married too. They invited us to come along to a big wedding supper their families were having for them.

"After dinner, the guests decided to shivaree us. They created quite a ruckus, ringing cowbells and banging pots and pans. Some of the women treated Geneva and me to a ride around the house in a washtub, while the men made the poor fellows ride on poles. We all had a wonderful time and even spent the night there.

"My prince and I *did* live happily ever after. We celebrated 50 wonderful years together on April 8, 1994, and appropriately shared that day with Lee and Geneva Roberts, just as we had so many years earlier."

Like Sylvia's story, the memories in this chapter will take you back to the days when the horrors of war were often the prelude to chivalry, love and romance in the Good Old Days.

—Ken Tate

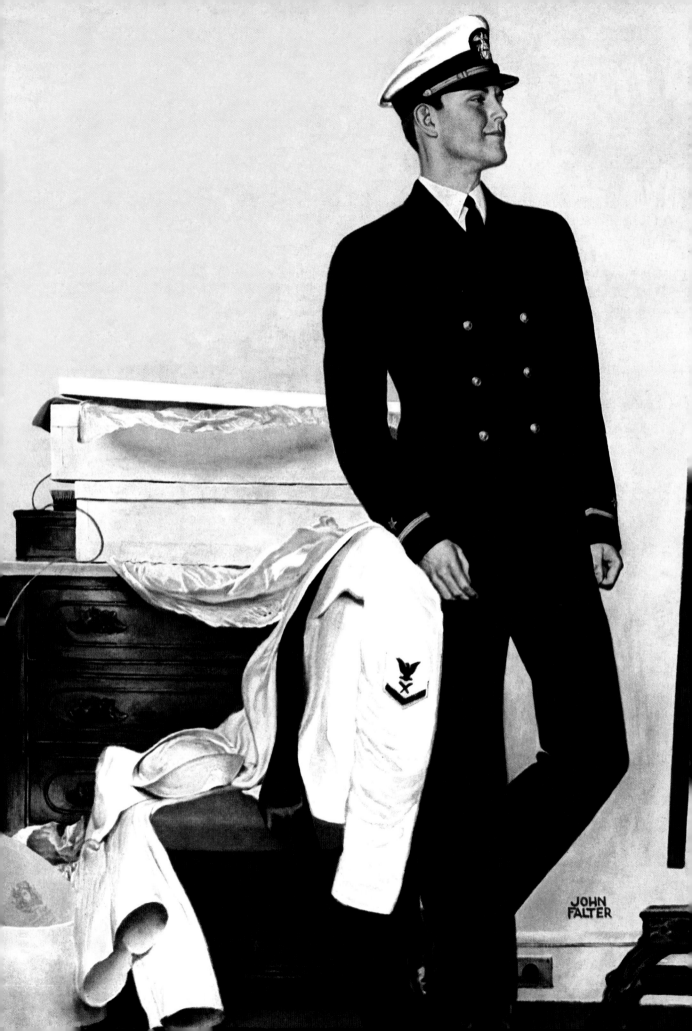

Wahi Pana

By Hertha "Bobbe" McKinney
as told to John J. Lesjack

Ensign William Russell McKinney of Springfield, Ohio, and I proudly announced our engagement in June 1941 at a private party in a friend's house in Waikiki, Territory of Hawaii. We received a raucous round of applause, probably because everyone at the party knew we had to wait a year to get married. Back then, Naval Academy graduates had agreed to wait for two years after graduating before saying "I do" with anyone.

However, Ensign McKinney—"Mac"—had other plans.

Hawaiians have a phrase that best describes my feelings about life in the islands. They call it *wahi pana,* which means "a storied place of myth and history."

My history with Mac began when we met at the Royal Hawaiian in Waikiki Beach. I was covering a story for the *Honolulu Star Bulletin.* A friend introduced us. He immediately enchanted me with his good looks, military bearing and politeness. The next thing I knew, we were walking barefoot on the beach. It was a storybook beginning for a kid from San Francisco, Calif., with only two years of college.

Our neighbor was yelling, "Look out at Pearl Harbor! Turn on your radio!"

Mac's first naval assignment was the USS *Oklahoma*, anchored out in Pearl Harbor.

That November, Mac came over to my apartment, got down on one knee and asked, "Bobbe, will you marry me?"

"Oh, yes!" I cried, and I wished I could call my mother.

A week later, we drove our Model A Ford out to a precious little church in Haleiwa, on the other side of the island from Honolulu. Mac wore a suit, and I wore a nice dress. The minister's wife and their Japanese gardener stood up for us. I kept any mention of our wedding out of the newspapers. We had a one-night honeymoon at the Haleiwa Hotel. Mac left for sea duty the next morning.

My life went back to its usual routine. One day, on assignment for the *Bulletin*, while Mac was out at sea, I flew a Piper Cub with a photographer to the island of Molokai and back.

On Dec. 6, 1941, I met my husband at Pearl Harbor. He had called and asked me to pick him up at the gate. I had no ID card yet, so I couldn't meet him where the liberty boat docked. When he showed up in his dress whites, he was so handsome.

He drove us over to the Pearl Harbor Officers' Club, a lovely old building with a long, wide lanai overlooking the harbor. We met with his friends and made plans to entertain everyone at our apartment that night. Then we drove out to Waikiki, had a swim, and met more friends at an elegant Chinese restaurant, Lau Yee Chai's, for dinner. We were happy being together.

Back at our apartment near Honolulu, we practiced the Hawaiian custom of removing our shoes before entering our residence. All the cadets thought it was a great custom. They enjoyed sitting shoeless on the *zabutons*—straw mats—on the floor.

Everyone left early enough that night to make the 12:30 a.m. liberty boat going back to the *Oklahoma*. Mac had traded duties with a class-mate who didn't have a date.

Sunday morning, we woke to a loud, insistent pounding on our front door. Our neighbor was yelling, "Look out at Pearl Harbor! Turn on your radio!"

We looked toward Pearl where the sky was all black. The radio tubes finally warmed up, and the announcer, Webley Edwards, said, "Pearl Harbor is being bombed!"

Before he left for his ship, Mac told me he would leave the car in the sugarcane field near Pearl. Would I ever see him again?

As I cleaned up the party mess, I heard Webley Edwards say, "Everyone listening should get in touch with their neighbors." My neighbors showed me the newspaper that said the *Oklahoma* had been the first ship sunk. All of our friends from the *Oklahoma* who had been at our party just a night earlier had gone down with the ship—including the classmate who had exchanged duties with Mac. I felt awful.

I tried calling our families on the main-land, but the lines were all jammed. In the afternoon, when I still had not heard from Mac, I had my neighbor drive me out to Pearl to get my car. After a brief search, I spotted our little "Green Hornet" deep in a sugarcane field. Other people were there getting their

cars too. Some nice man helped me pull my car out of the fields.

Once we got it on the road, we noticed bullet holes in the roof, but we saw no blood, so we reassured ourselves that everyone had gotten out safely.

Bobbe and her husband, Lt. j.g. McKinney, while visiting Annapolis after World War II.

Finally, late in the afternoon, I was able to get in a 3-minute call to the mainland to tell our families that Mac and I were safe, and that we had just been married. I was afraid of what they might think, but I believe they were so relieved that we were both safe that the other news didn't shock them too much.

Mac called on Tuesday. He needed an over-night kit. He was in Puuloa. I got everything together, plus some beer, and drove out to the cane fields 40 miles from town. We had just a few minutes together because I had to get back before blackout, but knowing he was safe made me feel better.

One Saturday afternoon, I drove out again for the opening of the "Officers' Club" in Puuloa; it was basically a tent with a working refrigerator. We were celebrating pretty well when we realized I would not have time to get back to town before blackout. Mac smuggled dinner for us from the mess tent.

During the night, I told Mac I had to use a bathroom—fast! "Our bathroom is called a 'head,' " Mac explained. But as he and his friends made arrangements to smuggle me in, general quarters sounded, and all hands dashed to their battle stations! I was told not to make any noise, or I might be shot! I was petrified! Finally the "all clear" was sounded, and I snuck into their "head," which still makes me giggle.

Sleeping two people in a one-man Army cot was very uncomfortable. At first light, I hid in the rumble seat of our Model A, and Mac drove us back to Pearl, said goodbye, and got a jeep ride back to the camp. I had a deep appreciation for my home after that long night.

Christmas was a bummer—barbed wire on Waikiki, martial law, and food and gasoline were

Author, Bobbe McKinney, prior to taking off on flight from Oahua to Molakai, with the Piper Cub used in her job.

rationed. But in April 1942, things got much better. Mac's promotion to lieutenant, junior grade, came through, and that automatically nullified the two-year wait on marriages. We went right down to the YMCA and stood in a long line to get married again! He wore his dress whites, and I wore a nice dress. Best of all, I got to call home and tell my mother!

Two months later, Mac and I left Hawaii aboard a Military Sea Transportation Service (MSTS) freighter that traveled with one destroyer escort. Mac had presented me with a beautiful fresh lei. The custom for people who want to return to the islands is to throw their lei overboard as they leave. So, as we rounded Diamond Head, I tossed my lei into the blue waters of the Pacific and prayed that the war would end soon.

Once underway, the captain asked for volunteers to stand watch. His crew had been standing watch around the clock on the way over, and they were exhausted. I'm proud to say that this Navy officer's wife stood her first watch aboard that ship!

Thirty years, two children and two grandchildren later, Mac retired from the Navy as a much-decorated admiral, and we did return to the islands. We had storybook lives, full of myth and history and adventure, for which I am most grateful. ❖

Tearful Goodbyes

By Warren Dowling

I first met Veetrice Mote in 1939. She attended the high school at Vici, Okla., and I went to Sharon, Okla., just 10 miles away. We dated off and on for about a year. At first, I think, neither of us was very impressed with the other. We both dated other people, but it never seemed to work out.

One day in 1940, I drove by her Aunt Pearl's home in Woodward, Okla., and there she was, in a swing on the front porch. I drove around the block and stopped and talked to her.

We found we had both just broken up with someone else. I asked her for a date that night, and she accepted. At that point, we started dating on a steady basis. We had never talked of marriage, but I am sure we had both thought of it.

Then came the day that all of my generation will remember forever. The Japanese dropped bombs on Pearl Harbor, starting a war that was to last for four years. All our lives had to be put on hold. My brother, Lester, was already in the Navy, and my friends were all talking about going into some branch of the military. I just couldn't wait to be a part of the Armed Forces that were going to defeat the Japanese and Germans.

The war was to last for four years. All our lives had to be put on hold.

On Jan. 4, 1942, Veetrice and I said the first of many goodbyes, and I boarded a bus for Oklahoma City. I intended to join the Navy like my brother, who was serving in the Pacific aboard the cruiser Houston. But when I lined up to be inducted, I was told that they had as many as could be processed that day, and I should come back the next day. Instead, I walked down the hall and signed up with the Air Force.

I received my basic training at Shepard Field, Texas, near Abilene, and was assigned to the First Fighter Control Squadron. We ended up as part of the Los Angeles Air Defense.

It was a new outfit, so promotions came fast. We got to Los Angeles in March 1942. By July, I was a staff sergeant. Any soldier who was married could live off the base with his commanding officer's permission. A staff sergeant or above could be paid rations and quarters. With that and my staff sergeant pay, I felt I could support Veetrice.

I proposed by mail, and she accepted the same way. Then I sent her an engagement ring. In September 1942, she got a ride to Los Angeles with her brother, John Mote, and his wife, Pauline.

On Sept. 7, 1942, Veetrice Mote became Veetrice Mote Dowling. We were married in a Baptist church in Bell, Calif., a suburb of Los Angeles. She wore a simple dress, and I was in my uniform. Attending the wedding were the pastor and his wife, our sister-in-law, Pauline Mote, and her friend. Our marriage lasted 47 years, until Veetrice's death.

As anyone who was married in the service can attest, housing was hard to come by around service bases, both because of the price and scarcity of facilities. The best we could come up with was a single room. It wasn't a boarding-house where we were fed, but a rooming house with sleeping quarters only. Veetrice ate at a café across the street, and I ate at the base.

That didn't last but a couple of months. Vee-trice got a job at Douglas Aircraft Co. and became "Rosie the Riveter." By combining our paychecks, we could afford a fur-nished apartment.

I would say that the year we spent in Los Angeles was the best year of our lives. For the first time, we had a little money to spend. In Oklahoma, the two most interesting things to do were washing clothes and watching the grass grow. But now we were in a huge city, with the ocean on one side and the mountains on the other. We bought a Model A Ford and took full advantage of all the sights.

When people think of Los Angeles today, they see eight-lane freeways with heavy, bumper-to-bumper traffic. But it wasn't that way back in 1942 and '43, when we lived there. There wasn't much traffic due to gas rationing, and we could ride the streetcars for a nickel.

Los Angeles was bordered by orange groves and was, to us, a beautiful city. With the street-car and our Model A, we spent our time going to the beach, mountains, amusement parks and museums. All such attractions were nonexistent where we had been raised.

About July 1943, we began to hear rumors about my outfit going overseas. Everyone who wanted a two-week furlough was given one.

Wedding day for Warren Dowling and Veetrice Mote in Los Angeles, 1942.

Veetrice and I took our Model A and went back to Oklahoma to see all our friends and relatives.

When we got back to the base, I was told that my outfit had moved to March Field about 60 miles away to begin training for overseas duty. I drove back and forth from our apartment for a few days, but it sure didn't take long for us to see that that wouldn't work. Between my duties in the service and driving 60 miles one way, I was only getting a few hours' sleep.

So we checked out of the apartment and put everything we owned in the car. Then Veetrice took me to March Field.

The nearest town, Riverside, Calif., had a population of 25,000, and it was surrounded by ser-vice bases where there were 100,000 troops. When she dropped me off at the gate that morning, we didn't know if she could find a place to live. But by the time I met her at the gate that night, she had found us a room much like we had had in Los Angeles—a sin-gle bedroom furnished only with a bed, clothes closet and dresser.

If it sounds like we had it rough, we had no regrets. We were very much in love and willing to pay any price to be togeth-er. At least we found a place to live. I know of other couples who found nothing and ended up with the wife being sent home by the Red Cross.

We lived in Riverside for about two months. Then, one night, I came home and told Veetrice that I was shipping out the next day. The next day we said another goodbye, and I was gone. I will always remember her standing in the drive-way, waving me a tearful goodbye.

We did not know where I was going or for how long. It turned out that I would be in the South Pacific for two years. ❖

I Was a Pilot's Wife

By Kathryn W. Smith

I was living in San Francisco, just two blocks from the Pacific Ocean, on Moraga Street. In the late 1930s and early 1940s, things were getting scarce in the clothing and food market. There was talk of rationing, which became a reality after Pearl Harbor. People began hoarding. They bought anything and everything: canned goods, sugar, coffee, meat, gasoline, shoes and tires, which were rationed. We carried our precious ration books with us at all times so they wouldn't be stolen.

Soon after Pearl Harbor, the streets of downtown San Francisco seemed almost empty of men. Japanese families were removed from the city to hastily built barracks at Tanforan, south of San Francisco.

I was working nights for a large law firm in San Francisco. The only other member of the night force was Gladys Cox. Our office was on the 19th floor of the Standard Oil Building on Bush Street, with a view of the Bay. The windows were blacked out. If we heard a siren, we were to turn off the lights entirely and go to the second floor. But we were at the mercy of the night watchman. Sometimes he forgot us, and we had no elevator, and the doors on the stairways were locked. If that happened, we just stayed put.

One night I saw five crashes. I didn't sleep well that night.

We had a half hour for dinner, and if we left the building, we always told the watchman where we were going. One night we were having a sandwich in an Owl Drugstore when the siren sounded. The restaurant turned off the lights and told everyone to stay, but after a half hour, Gladys and I decided to leave. We placed money on the counter and walked the three blocks to the Standard Oil Building in the pitch-black darkness, with no sound anywhere. Everything had stopped. It was weird!

The watchman was waiting for us in front of the building. He took us to the second floor to an unlighted room filled with people. We stayed there for two hours before the all-clear siren sounded.

All streetlights were blackened on the side toward the bay and the ocean, and those not entirely blacked out were dim. My home was almost at the ocean, so it was even darker at home.

I had a "B" ration stamp for gas because I lived so far from work, and no taxi would go that far unless they had a full load both ways.

One night when the moon was out, I drove to the beach and then along the ocean to my home. It was exceptionally beautiful, and the ocean was shining in the light of the moon. But also visible was a large convoy of our ships leaving San Francisco. They were unlighted, but the moonlight made them targets.

I had black shades on all my windows at home, and the small light over the house number was turned off. No one was allowed to light a cigarette or even smoke one outdoors at night. Even that small light could be seen from a great distance in the air.

When the siren sounded at night, we sat on the steps and watched what was happening. Airplanes flew right over us, with beams of light from the lookouts on the beach holding them in sight. The first time we saw the planes was shortly after the Ellwood, Calif., oilfield shelling by an enemy submarine, and it was suspected that the ones flying over our coastline could be enemy planes.

On the street behind my home there was an old, two-story house on a small knoll. It had attic windows that faced the ocean, and someone had been sending light signals from those windows to someone in the air. I reported this to Gene, our Civil Defense volunteer, and he reported it to the FBI. The people were soon removed from the house, and it was padlocked and guarded.

One Sunday morning, I was sitting in the backyard, reading the paper, when I heard the *tap-tap* of a telegraph key. I looked over the fence and saw a man at a desk in his garage, tapping out a message. As I listened, he soon gave longitude and latitude messages over a ham radio or phone—he was speaking, not tapping.

I reported the telegraph tapping and the radio messages. The FBI said they had this particular house under surveillance, along with a number of others in our area. They thanked me for being alert and calling them. I never learned the results of my efforts.

Orland Smith, my future husband, was drafted in the spring of 1942. We had planned to be married as soon as we could, but he was transferred several times before he finally was sent to Del Rio, Texas. I got a leave of absence and took the train to Del Rio, the end of nowhere, 3 miles from the Mexican border. The only thing Del Rio was noted for was a high-powered radio station owned and operated by Dr. Brinkley. Dr. Brinkley owned practically everything in town.

When I stepped off the train in Del Rio, the porter asked me if I was sure this was where I was supposed to get off. When I was in my hotel room, I called the operator and asked if she could reach Orland on the field. She did, and we made our date to get the marriage license; however, I had to do it alone, because his leave started too late.

The county clerk's office was filled with Mexicans from Villa Acuna. I think I was the only American in the place, except for the clerk and his assistant. I waited in line, and the people in front of me, a young couple from Mexico, wanted a marriage license. The clerk asked them their age and if they had their parents' consent, then handed them a paper for their parents to sign.

The author's husband flew a B-26 bomber like these in World War II. Photo courtesy the U.S. Air Force Museum.

I was next, and the clerk wanted to talk. The new field was bringing about 4,200 soldiers in, and it was an exciting time for this little border town. I explained why I was there alone, and he said he'd help us get married. He told me to go to his hotel, the St. Charles on Main Street, and when Orland arrived, he'd take us to the judge. He handed me a paper and I left.

When Orland arrived at the Roswell Hotel, after a few hugs and kisses, we looked at the license. It was a "Consent of Parents for Minors to Wed" form. We had a good laugh over that and then phoned the clerk and told him of his mistake. He met us at his hotel, and then we went to the courthouse where he issued a proper license.

He then said Orland would have to have a physical; it was required before we could be married. He saw his doctor friend playing pool. A physical in a pool hall? The doctor looked at Orland and asked, "You're in the Army?"

"Yes," Orland answered, "in the Air Force."

The doctor said, "If you are, your health is OK." He gave us the certificate we needed.

The clerk drove us to the judge's home on the outskirts of town. The judge's wife answered the door, and our wedding was put on hold until the Judge's favorite radio program, *Fibber McGee and Molly*, was finished. We sat in the hallway and waited impatiently with the clerk.

Eventually the program ended, and with the judge's wife and the clerk as our witnesses, we were duly married. The clerk took us back to town. He said that ours was the first of many marriages that would probably take place as soon as the field was officially open.

We had almost two weeks together. When I returned to the San Francisco financial district to work, I noticed many changes. Ships were coming into the Bay with gaping holes in their sides, or the bow blown off, the ship listing to one side. These were headed for Hunters' Point Shipyards for repairs.

Other ships with red crosses painted on both sides and on the deck were bringing the wounded home. The Southern Pacific train, all cars painted with long white stripes and red crosses,

When the siren sounded at night, we sat on the steps and watched.

met the boats. The badly wounded were taken immediately to Dibble Hospital in Palo Alto on Middlefield Road. They had a spur track right at the hospital entrance. As soldiers were able to be moved, they were transferred to hospitals all over the country, near their homes, if possible, which made room for the next trainload.

One of my friends was a nurse who worked with these men. She was injured while bringing home a planeload of wounded men from the South Pacific. The plane was shot down and a piece of metal went through her throat, and she was unable to speak for several years. Later, she often spoke of the courage of the men. "It was something unbelievable unless you witnessed it," she said. Those who knew her said that she had the same kind of courage.

When Orland knew that Laughlin Field would be his permanent base, he asked me to come down and work there. From the room I rented, I saw the flares of crashed planes, and it wasn't very reassuring. Orland was flying almost every day, many times at night or on instruments only. There was no way I could learn what was happening until he came to town at night. One night I saw five crashes. I didn't sleep well that night.

Soon D-Day was a reality. Ten pilots returned after serving their 50 missions in Europe and made up the Test Flight. Orland was their engineer and co-pilot. They had their accidents too. One Sunday, one of them took a plane up for a test, and when we heard it, we knew it was headed for a crash. One engine fell off and went through a house in the row behind ours as the people hurried out the other door. The pilot's life was lost. It was a very sad day.

The field was getting ready to close. Orland was sent to Kern, Utah, and ended up in Wichita Falls. After a week, it was back to California and finally home in April 1946.

When I look back on our war experiences, I remember all the kindnesses extended to us. We went back in the 1950s and visited many of the friends we had made then. The B-26 bomber changed Orland's whole future. He worked for United Airlines until he died in 1981. ❖

Clara's Soldier Boy

By Audrey Corn

I admired my big cousin, Clara, and I wanted to do everything Clara did. But Mama said that I was too little to write to a soldier boy back in the 1940s when I was growing up in Brooklyn, N.Y.

Clara had just started high school, and when a Red Cross volunteer addressed the opening assembly, Clara listened carefully. The volunteer urged the students—particularly the girls—to write letters to the troops overseas.

Clara wanted to help in the war effort. However, she was only 14, so she didn't have a boyfriend in the service to write to like the girls in the upper grades did.

But Mama said that Clara could still help out. "Write to Cousin Bill," she suggested.

The Red Cross volunteer had emphasized that our boys needed cheering up, so Clara sent Bill an entertaining account of her recent activities with her friends. She didn't discuss family news, knowing that Bill's mother wrote to him daily.

Bill's mother gave Clara a general military address. From there, the mail was sorted and sent to the men. Millions of letters went out, and mix-ups were bound to occur. Maybe the last name on Clara's envelope got torn or smudged. Maybe someone misread it. Anyhow, at mail call, Clara's letter wound up in the hands of the wrong Bill.

The new Bill had never met Clara; he must have wondered why she expected him to remember the names of certain people and places. But it was wartime, and he was lonely, so he replied with a friendly note of his own.

Cousin Bill knew Clara was only 14. The new Bill assumed that Clara was older—and Clara rather enjoyed his mistake. She also enjoyed the envious looks she got from her girlfriends when she showed them the photo of her handsome soldier boy that he had sent with his note.

Auntie didn't want Clara to correspond with an older man. But Clara countered by asking what harm could come from writing to a homesick GI on the other side of the world. And so the letters flew back and forth, and everything was hunky-dory, as we said back in the '40s.

Then the soldier boy wrote that he was coming home and couldn't wait to renew his acquaintance with Clara! The new Bill lived in Connecticut. He planned to take a bus to Manhattan and then ride the subway to Brooklyn.

But Auntie vetoed the plan. She said that it did not matter that Clara had turned 15. Clara was still too young to date a 19-almost-20-year-old man—and a stranger to boot!

> *Auntie didn't want Clara to correspond with an older man.*

Clara's friends told Clara to write that she was "going steady." But my cousin didn't lie to her soldier boy. His letters had shown him to be a decent, honorable young man. She chose to tell the truth—at least enough of the truth to spare Bill's feelings and still protect her pride.

It was a difficult letter to compose. She said that her parents were very strict. They would only let her date men from her church or local neighborhood, men whose parents they already knew. This was all true enough. Clara crossed her fingers and mailed her letter.

My cousin was a good judge of character, even at the tender age of 15. Bill wrote back saying that he respected her parents' wishes. He thanked Clara for her letters and her cookies, and for making his tour of duty easier to bear.

Clara breathed a sigh of relief. Truth be told, she wasn't ready to date a 19-almost-20-year-old soldier boy from Connecticut.

God smiled on my cousin and me and all of our generation. He gave us parents who set laws and limits. We were lucky to have mothers and fathers who took care of us and guided us back in the Good Old Days. ❖

Bye-Bye, Biloxi

By Marjory Horst

"Bye-bye, Biloxi," I said, slamming down the trunk of our old 1939 Studebaker. "It's been fun." One last check of our temporary home and we'd be gone. Nearby, my landlady observed—scowling, not happy. For enlisted men's families, life in Biloxi, Miss., in 1944 wasn't exactly the American dream. Oh, the town had typical Southern charm along what is now Interstate 90. To the north imposing mansions hid behind huge trees, seductively veiled in Spanish moss. Scattered along were hotels, stores and restaurants—one featuring Northern-fried chicken.

To the south, the gulf waters beckoned bathers and fishermen. The beach was fabulous and the people nice, but the town was overcrowded, housing was scarce and our subsistence pay didn't quite cut it.

Some men could live on base, but Uncle Sam felt families didn't belong there. He was right. Nevertheless, there we were—camp followers—most married, some with small children, others, like me, awaiting the birth of a child.

Our men were "Permanent Party," buck privates, PFCs and corporals—service personnel. Little did we know "permanent" to the Air Force meant six weeks to six months. We learned. Soon many husbands were ordered to Santa Ana Air Force Base near Los Angeles, leaving by troop train—10 August 1944, 0600 hours.

Our baby arrived early, and we joined those waving goodbye, optimistically expecting to leave shortly ourselves. We later found this was easier said than done.

"No!" the medical officer thundered in response to requests for reassignment of my base pass, commissary card and gas stamps to California. "You're not supposed to be driving yet. You don't belong here, and you don't belong

1938 *Farmer's Wife*, House of White Birches nostalgia archives

there either. Take the train to Ohio. That baby needs a home."

"But our car, our stuff!"

He patted my hand. "Look, I can get you stamps for Ohio, but not the rest. You're not even supposed to be on base except for medical purposes."

I left, clutching the baby and the prized gas stamps. Not willing to take no for an answer, I was soon burning up the lines between Biloxi, Bedford and Massillon, Ohio, and Santa Ana. By whatever worked—begging, cajoling or crying—I soon accumulated stamps. Tractor stamps came from my in-laws on the farm, some from my parents, and a few from a kind trucker, touched by my plight.

Thus I found myself, in mid-September, ready to roll. We sped west at 35 mph, the maximum for our balding recaps and gas conservation. Our daughter slept quietly until 4 in the afternoon, when I heard warning signals from the back, indicating hunger. *Good timing*, I thought, pulling off the road in a shaded spot.

Reaching for the basket, I was startled by a sharp *pop!*, then a hissing sound as the car settled. Oh, no! I'd thought of flats, but not here, miles from anywhere.

First things first, I told myself, changing, feeding and burping the baby, then tucking her back in. Changing tires was not my thing, but I'd have to do it, get help or walk.

Somebody will come, I thought, ignoring approaching dusk and sparse traffic due to the gas shortage. Meanwhile, action, please …

Hearing an approaching car, I snatched the baby, stood by the road and waved. It sped by without a glance, followed by another, whose occupants smiled and waved, but continued. Discouraged, I returned to my task.

The spare tire, I knew, was on the bottom. Pulling out the jack and tire iron, I was dismayed to find this jack had no handle. I'd watched my husband change tires, and I didn't think it looked too difficult, but his jack had a handle.

As I dug deeper, I heard another car. To my relief, this one slowed and stopped. Out stepped a handsome officer in full-dress uniform, complete with shiny new wings.

"Need some help?" he inquired.

"Do I ever!" I replied.

He made quick work of finding and inserting the jack handle. Then he changed the tired, repacked the trunk and was on his way, telling me he was on compassionate leave, taking his family home before going overseas. I wished him luck and happy landings.

Behind schedule, we now needed a new tire as well as lodging. A room was no problem; the tire was more of a challenge. I knew they were available with a ration stamp, extra money or the right friends. I struck out on all counts. The first attendant I approached said they had none. Those I noticed he said were sold.

"Keesler Field!" we shouted. It was like finding a long-lost pal.

Forming another plan, I dined at a nearby restaurant, where I struck up a conversation with a waitress who directed me to a smaller garage. "Steer clear of the big places," she advised.

Gathering up our sleeping child, I approached the mechanic working there, and in a quavering voice, explained I had no stamp, but desperately needed a tire.

"We can't sell 'em without a stamp, ma'am. It's against the law," he said. "Sorry."

As he turned away, I quickly I loosened the baby's blanket, removed her bootie and gave her a sharp flick on the foot. On cue, my little doll responded with a howl of outrage. Startled, the man turned back, and then said, "Just a minute, I'll ask." I then heard him say, "Joe, there's a soldier's wife out here with a tiny baby, and it's crying. Can we … ?"

He soon returned saying he'd fix it. Saved by the yell! "Sorry, sweetie," I whispered, "Mommy had to do that."

As I handed over the money, the manager observed with a smile, "You got a mighty nice baby, ma'am," then added with a wink, "and you're sure getting good mileage outta that tractor."

Next day, somewhere in Texas, another tire blew, exploding with a loud noise, sending the car careening into a field. Comforting our crying child, I surveyed the damage. Poor old Studey was a sad sight, with a rear tire shredded.

Suddenly I heard a tractor. Turning, I found myself looking up at a tall, smiling man. "Looks like we got a little problem here," he drawled.

Bless all Texans! He solved my little problem by taking me home where I had a substantial lunch while his lovely wife held, fed and admired our baby, and he repaired the car. How he managed all this, I had no idea and didn't ask. All I know for sure is we were on our way again in a few hours.

We drove on, marveling at the endless sweep of land and sky of this vast countryside. Buzzing along, I noticed a serviceman close to the road, thumb upraised. Slowing, I quickly recognized the familiar blue patch with embroidered wings and the caption "Keesler Field, Biloxi, Mississippi." Running to the car, he spotted the matching decal. "Keesler Field!" we shouted. It was like finding a long-lost pal, though we'd never met.

Friendships blossomed rapidly then. I learned his name was Gene, a sergeant/drill instructor, on his way home to Anaheim for his wedding before shipping overseas.

We joined forces, and after another flat tire, a serious discussion about finances and an all-night drive, we arrived in Tucson, Ariz., planning to stop and visit a former neighbor. She welcomed us, providing rest, food, showers and laundry facilities. As we were leaving, she mentioned she'd be sure to tell my mother about my nice male traveling companion—with emphasis on *male*! Oh well.

Reputations ruined, we crossed the desert at night—for our own comfort and the safety of fragile tires—arriving in Palm Springs at dawn, then on to Anaheim. With many thanks and good wishes, I dropped Gene off at his home, just hours before the scheduled wedding.

On my own again, I headed south, nearing journey's end, I thought. Ironically, after finding my way this far, I got lost between Anaheim and Santa Ana, and I arrived late in the afternoon.

Phoning my anxious husband who was standing by with final directions, and finding myself drained and exhausted, I wailed, "We're here, and I'm tired of driving. If you want us, come and get us!" He did. ❖

Takin' a Chance

By Elizabeth Bowman Good

While my sister Ruth's husband was in the Pacific, she lived in San Diego, Calif., next door to Mrs. Gayle Tweed. Upon learning that Ruth had a sister in high school and Gayle a brother in the Air Force, they decided that it would be nice if these two wrote to each other. Gayle gave my sister a picture of Sie to send to me, and Ruth gave her one of me to send to Sie. Having done their duty, they left the rest to us and to fate.

Sie and I were receptive to this, and we wrote to each other for the rest of the war. We sent pictures and shared our hopes and dreams for when our world was at peace.

I didn't make any concrete plans, but Sie was thinking of the kind of wife he would need. He hoped to rent his parents' farm, and he needed a farm girl. It occurred to Sie that his Arkie girl might just be the one he was looking for.

He asked that I use the money he sent to buy a ring—not an engagement ring, but a small diamond promise one, meaning that I would not marry another until the two of us met. I had no serious boyfriend, so I bought a dainty little diamond ring for $75.

Sie was discharged in the fall of 1945. He arrived at our house on Dec. 1. I met him at the door with a hug and a kiss. Mama gave him a warm, friendly smile. But my father only grunted a chilly hello before starting his inquisition. Sie laid out his life's history on the dining table for my father.

Sie proposed to me on Dec. 2, and we were married in Marianna on the 11th, my 20th birthday. We spent our brief honeymoon in Memphis. We returned to Moro the following day, packed my things, and left for Washington on the 13th.

Our life has been a pleasant one, and we feel the Lord blessed us by giving us the opportunity of takin' a chance on love. ❖

Wartime Thanksgiving

By Alomo Leslie McElmurray

*B*am! I tried to staple my thumb to the tally sheet, though not intentionally. I stood there, sore thumb in my mouth, rummaging in the drawer with my other hand to find a Band-Aid to keep from bleeding all over my work. I was fighting back tears when a knock sounded on the window of my teller's cage.

Tears had been close to the surface all day. I was thankful that my family wanted me back home for the duration of the war, and I was grateful to be back at my job in the National Bank of Commerce in Memphis, Tenn., but tomorrow was Thanksgiving and I was sure my husband, Rex, wouldn't be having Thanksgiving. He was in a prisoner-of-war camp in Germany.

With my return home, Mom had perked up. But now she was depressed because she couldn't provide our usual Thanksgiving feast. Meat was strictly rationed, and our family didn't buy black market. All week she had tried to get me to help with the menu. But I couldn't talk to her about food. All I could think of was Rex.

This day had been especially tiring. Preholiday business was heavy, and I had waited on both the Yellow Cab and the Frisco Railroad accounts. Their deposits were huge. During World War II, few private cars qualified for gas ration stamps.

It was late, and now someone was knocking on my window. I unlatched the frosted glass window and there stood Mr. E.E. Buxton, a director of the bank. He motioned for me to raise the bars so he could shove something into the opening.

Mr. Buxton was the epitome of the rich eccentric. Standing there in his baggy corduroy pants, flannel shirt and slouchy old hunting hat, Mr. Buxton didn't appear to be one of the richest men in town—but he was.

I knew Mr. Buxton was unpredictable, but the sight of four yellow, scaly legs followed by the bodies of two plump geese covered with cream and brown feathers left me gasping. Mr. Buxton had been hunting, a luxury few could afford in wartime. He hadn't said a word to me, and by the time I regrouped and looked up, he had already crossed the lobby and was quickly shuffling into the boardroom, a place off-limits to lowly employees like me.

After I balanced, I scurried to the bus stop. The 5 o'clock office workers had crowded on ahead of me, but I pushed my way on. There I stood, my purse draped over one shoulder, holding the strap overhead with one hand and the string handle around the geese's feet with the other.

Perhaps I looked like a laughingstock, but many were envious of my two plump geese. They were heavy, and by the time I got a seat, my hand was almost paralyzed.

Finally, the bus came to my stop. I still had two blocks to walk. As the geese got heavier, I swapped them from hand to hand, and I stopped to rest about every third house—that is, until the dog joined us. He didn't attack, but he sure eyed my burden. My pace quickened, and there were no more rest stops.

"Here's our Thanksgiving dinner!" I called to Mom as I entered the kitchen. But she had a surprise for me too. The mailman had left a bundle of seven letters from Rex. The letters were heavily censored, but the last one was almost up-to-date. Rex was alive and well, and Mom had her Thanksgiving dinner supplies.

Several months later, the horrible war was over. Rex came home, thin and pale, but eager for the future. Thanksgiving Day—in 1944 and every year since—has been a special time for giving thanks at our home. ❖

The mailman had left a bundle of seven letters from Rex.

War and Love

By Angela Scalzitti McCrea

I must say that the World War II years were the happiest years of my life. I was a savings teller at the South Chicago Bank on the South Side of Chicago. Many soldiers, sailors and Marines lived in our neighborhood. When their allotment checks came into the bank for deposit, my friend, Ann, the teller next to me, and I would post the checks into their savings accounts.

When I sent them their receipts, I always added a PS. wishing them safety and assuring them they were in my prayers, hoping for the war to end and for a quick return home. When a sailor, soldier or Marine came home on furlough, naturally he would come to the bank looking for me. Ann and I had many dates during those days.

One day, a Mrs. McCrea came to my window with the allotment checks from her three sons, James, John and Justin. I recognized James as Jim McCrea, whom I knew from school at Bowen High. He was a year ahead of me, and to tell the truth, I didn't like him. I thought he acted conceited.

He was in drama, acted in many plays and was editor-in-chief of the school newspaper, *The Bowen Arrow*.

I mentioned to his mother that I knew of him. A few minutes after she left the bank, she was back at my window, insisting that I give her my address so Jim and I could write to each other. She didn't know I had about 25 guys already on my list.

A week later, I received his first letter. He told me he was on his way overseas and would write to me from wherever he would be. He landed in the Aleutian Islands and participated in the battle of Attu.

We wrote to each other for two and half years, all the time he was there. During that time, he became an Armed Forces Radio announcer known as "Genial Jim," the World War II version of *Good Morning, Vietnam*. He also trained a newcomer named Frank McGee, who later hosted *The Today Show*.

We fell in love through our letters. What a surprise it was when he called from California and said he would be home for Christmas and would be stationed somewhere in the United States!

I was so excited to know that we were going to meet for the first time. I opened the door on Christmas Eve, 1944. We took one look at each other and kissed. At that moment, we both knew we were meant for each other.

This photo of the author and her husband-to-be was taken on April 24, 1945, the day before their wedding.

Our first date was midnight Mass at Sts. Peter and Paul Church. We became engaged on Jan. 6, 1945, and were married during his next furlough, on April 25, 1945. The accompanying picture was taken by my sister, Lida, the day before we were married.

He was discharged in January 1946 after serving four years and nine months.

We had three wonderful children, Judy, Philip and Kevin. We had a very happy life until he passed away on Jan. 16, 1979. ❖

Bread on a Thread

By Faith Schremp

*I*n 1925, Mama taught me to sew. I was 4 years old. My first project was a tea apron for my great-grandmother. I was thrilled that she considered me grown up enough to do it. Mama had been a dressmaker before marrying Daddy, and she had made all our clothes as well as our curtains, quilts and dish towels. This day was bright and sunny, just made for playing outside in the sandpile. But for the moment at least, I was much too old for such pastimes. When my younger sister and brother waited for me to join them, I told them, "You kidlets run along and play in the sand. Today us big kids are going to sew!"

My heart swelled with pride as my mother spread the blue-checked gingham on the table, letting me run my fingers over it, feeling the texture and smelling the newness of it.

The author and her husband, Butch, soon after their marriage.

She held my hand on the scissors as we cut one strip 4 inches wide for the waistband, extending into strings to tie behind Great-Grandma's back. Then we cut a square for the front and two small squares for pockets. I was enthralled; I'd never cut cloth before, only paper.

Then Mama sat me down by the window and brought needle and white thread. She showed me how to thread the needle and tie a double knot in the end so I wouldn't lose my thread as I pulled it through.

I watched intently as she basted the long strip to the front square, running a gathering thread across the top so the apron would fall into soft ripples across Great-Grandma's ample tummy. Mama pinned and basted the pockets in place, and it was time for me to begin.

She showed me how to make tiny running stitches to fasten the long strip in place on the gathers. I struggled to do what she did, pricking my fingers so many times that the blood oozed out and I began to cry. "Maybe she's too young for that," Daddy remarked, looking sorry for me.

"No, she can learn this now," Mama said, "and practice makes perfect!" With only this much experience, I was already beginning to have doubts about how exciting it would be to learn to sew. Suddenly the sandbox was calling me back to my childhood. "I wanna go and play, Mama," I said plaintively.

But she was firm. "We're not quitters. We don't give up just because something isn't easy. We keep trying until we get clear across the top. Then we can put it away until tomorrow, and you may play."

I tried again, but with the same results. As the days went by and I struggled to do a few inches more, that simple apron took on the dimensions of a monster! I wished I had never started it!

Every time I sewed crooked or did anything less than perfect, Mama ripped it out, and I had to do it over. I grew to hate the sight and feel and smell of that apron! I hated needles! They were mean! Thread tangled and aggravated me, and all that time I was spending on an apron, my little brother and sister were in the sandbox, carefree and happy.

Well, it took the better part of the summer to finish the simple, gathered, blue-checked gingham apron. Although every stitch was in place, and it looked very elegant, I knew I would always hate sewing.

There were many more projects while I was growing up, with Mama insisting on perfection. If I wanted new clothes, I was told I was perfectly capable of making them, and that was my only way of getting them.

Mama taught me the blind stitch, backstitch, chain stitch and numerous others besides all those aggravating but beautiful embroidery stitches. Then there were knitting and crocheting.

Years later, during World War II, I married my high-school sweetheart, determining to stay near him wherever he landed until he shipped overseas to participate in the Normandy Invasion on D-Day.

On soldier's pay I could not stay. I had to find work. I looked for work in nearby towns, but natives resented the invasion of military dependents and hired local people where they could. I could understand their attitude, but I needed work.

One day, the tailor from the PX in my husband's camp approached me. He needed help, and he had heard I could sew. It was the last thing in the world I wanted to do! I would have taken waitress work or factory work or almost anything else! But this was my opportunity to be near my husband as long as he was there, so I took the job, sewing chevrons and stripes onto Army shirts and blouses, braid onto overseas caps, and buttons onto a general's overcoat. And I made many too-big GI uniforms fit the trim bodies of our fighting men.

Truly I was earning my bread with a bit of thread, and I thanked God Mama had made me learn to sew! ❖

1935 *Household Magazine*, House of White Birches nostalgia archives

War Bride

By Anna B. Loudermilk

While on vacation this year, I found some cassette tapes of songs that were played during World War II. As I listened, the memories flooded back to the days I spent in Camp Blanding, Fla. I was a young war bride. Talmage Loudermilk and I were married on April 22, 1944. Just returning from a tour of duty in the Canal Zone as a member of the jungle platoon, he was assigned to Camp Blanding, Fla., where he was attached to Company E, 213th Training Battalion as a drill instructor. I joined him in July of that year.

There were guest houses on the base for wives and girlfriends who had come to visit their soldiers. The stay was limited to three days. After my stay ended at the guest house, I went to Jacksonville to find a room.

I was from a small town. I knew nothing about larger cities—especially about how to go about finding a room. I was blessed, for I saw a "Room for Rent" sign just before the olive green camp bus pulled into the Camp Blanding bus station in Jacksonville.

> *Talmage heard a murmur drifting back through the troops: "That was his wife."*

Because of Talmage's duties as a drill instructor, I saw him only once or twice a week. To say I was homesick was an understatement. Finally we decided that it was best for me to move out to the base and stay in the dormitory.

It was while living at the dormitory that I had my first experience with hurricanes. I was awakened one morning by one of the other girls who lived there. "Go to the dayroom," she said. "A hurricane is coming."

I slipped on my dress and shower clogs, and hurridly started for the dayroom. The wind was so strong that it nearly blew me off the sidewalk.

The other girls had already gathered in the dayroom. Some of them were so frightened that they had turned a couch over and lay behind it. Others gathered in small groups.

Every hour or so, a captain would come into the room and say something like this: "The hurricane is coming, and it is coming at 90 miles an hour."

I found a sheet of paper and wrote my mother a letter. At the top I wrote, "If you receive this letter, then you will know that I am all right."

As it turned out, the worst of the hurricane went around us. We were left with extremely high winds and heavy rains.

I lived at the dorm until Talmage and I found a place to live a short distance from the camp in a place called Boom Town.

Camp Blanding, a hub of activity, was built around beautiful Kingsley Lake. It was said, "Kingsley Lake looks like a silver dollar from the air." It had beautiful beaches!

The main entrance was called Main B Gate. Here the MPs checked passes and identification. Troops often marched out through this entrance to the ranges and to bivouac. Close-order drilling was done inside the camp. The main streets were used to move troops from one range to another, as well as for regular traffic.

One evening I was on my way to the PX when I saw a platoon of soldiers marching down the street. It was my husband and a group of trainees. At the command "Eyes right," all eyes turned toward me. With another command, "Ready front," the men moved on down the street.

Talmage heard a murmur drifting back through the troops: "That was his wife."

I started working at the Main B PX just inside the main gate. "May I help you?" was the phrase of the day. It was a very busy place. In the evening, after duty, the soldiers streamed through the doors. They were relaxed, joking, laughing and flirting with the girls. They splurged on cigarettes, ice cream, candy, hot dogs and drinks.

I worked the clothing counter. We sold everything from chevrons to tennis balls. Across the aisle, the soldiers picked up personal items and lingered over the jewelry counter.

All the while, the jukebox belted out songs such as *Three Little Fishes, Rum and Coca-Cola* and *By the Light of the Silvery Moon.*

The beer garden was out in back of the PX. I could hear waves of laughter coming from the dimly lit garden. Men away from home and their loved ones were drowning their cares

Above: Talmage and Anna Loudermilk (left) with Virginia and Hugh Tuck (right) at Camp Blanding, Fla. Below: A copy of the Camp Blanding pass the author carried during those years.

1945 **CAMP BLANDING, FLORIDA**
Date 18 July 1944
Anna Belle Loudermilk
is the _____ wife _____ of
Pfc. Talmage A. Loudermilk Asn 3411
and is permitted to enter Camp Blanding for the purpose of visiting the above named Office or Enlisted man.
By order of the Camp Commander

(CAMP PROVOST MARSHAL)

Requested by
Frederick D. Keeler
Capt. Inf.   3842 BENNING 1-15-44 10,000

for a little while. Service Club No. 1, a barbershop and a dry cleaner were also close by.

Time passed and I went to work at Dental Clinic No. 2. One young recruit who came to have some work done was from a small town in North Carolina. He must have been nervous, for the dentist—who was an officer—had to use more than the usual amount of Novocain to numb his gums.

When the lieutenant went to wash his hands, the young man asked me, "What did he do before he joined the Army?"

"He was a dentist," I replied.

"I didn't know," he replied. "He works as if he is working on a horse."

One soldier was waiting for the dentist to begin working on his teeth. When he opened his mouth, the lieutenant took one peek and said, "What are you trying to grow, a victory garden in your mouth?"

I was working at the clinic the day someone called out, "The war has ended!" The whole second floor erupted in a joyful cry. Such whooping and hollering! One lieutenant chased another around the sinks in the middle of the room and poured a pitcher of water on his head.

In 1996, on a trip to Florida to visit Hugh and Virginia Tuck—friends from Camp Blanding days—we once again toured the camp. Virginia had been a war bride also, and our friendship has spanned 58 years.

Camp Blanding has changed. The National Guard is now based there. Most of the buildings are gone, and the Main B PX has been remodeled. Service Club No. 1 is now an excellent World War II museum.

We lost contact with most of the friends we made at Camp Blanding. However, there are those we will never forget—people like Love, the mail clerk; Scott, another drill instructor; K.I. Stanley, and Capt. Frederick D. Kesler, among others.

Many years have passed. Even yet, I lean back in my old rocking chair and let my mind wander back to those sunny days in Camp Blanding.

In my memory, it will always be as it was in 1944 and 1945. ❖

Cupid Josie

By Barbara Leary

Being born in 1926 in a small Indiana town, I grew up in the Depression era. But I was entirely unaware that we were poor until our neighbors' daughter, almost four years younger than I was, began tagging after me. Her father was a rural mail carrier, and that was a very secure job at that time.

She was an only child, but her parents had taken in two nephews, 11 and 15, when their mother died. The younger boy was quite taken with his little girl cousin, and she adored him. He didn't exist in my world, being seven years my senior.

Then, suddenly, when I was 12 years old, he became very visible to this starry-eyed preteen. I had a crush on Hugh, Josie's smiling cousin! But I kept it mostly to myself.

The years passed, and Hugh went into the service during World War II. I was busy enjoying my high school years and was all but engaged to a nice young man I'd dated prior to his entering the service.

When Hugh went overseas, I was encouraged to write to him, which I did. By this time, I had graduated from high school and was working in Indianapolis. In late summer of 1944, Hugh returned to the states as an Officer Candidate School candidate. When he arrived home, Josie called and invited me to come and help welcome him back. She didn't have to ask a second time.

He finished his OCS training in late January 1945, and we were wed in February. I've always joked, "I started chasing him when I was 12 years old, and by the time I was 19, he had caught me!"

We had six children, raising five, and celebrated 55 years of marriage before he passed away following open-heart surgery.

Josie and I are still very close, keeping in touch by phone and letter. She truly was our Cupid! ❖

Pictures From Home

By Brenda Knable

*I*n 1942, my grandpa, Berendt Kappedal, left farm life behind in northern Minnesota and entered military service. He was stationed in Roseburg, Ore., far from family, friends and all things familiar.

He had been there for two years when he met my grandma, Earlamae Palmer. They met when Grandpa went into the malt shop where Grandma was working. He was twice her age—32 years to her 16. I'm sure that Grandpa probably turned on the dimples, which were his biggest asset. He had a certain charm! Apparently it was quite a whirlwind courtship. Two weeks after they met, they were married.

Unfortunately, there was a war going on, and Grandpa was called to serve overseas in the Pacific. Uncle Sam was no respecter of romance at that time, so Grandma was left behind in Oregon. She would not be alone for long, though, because nine months after she married Grandpa, along came their first son, Richard (my dad).

It couldn't have been easy for Grandpa, being on foreign soil, with a new wife and son back in the States, not knowing if he would make it home again. Added to his anxiety was the fact that they could not communicate with letters because Grandpa could not read!

Grandpa was a Norwegian, born into a farm family. As far back as I can remember, he had a thick accent. The farm was everything to him.

That was how he and his siblings had been raised. Education was not important.

Grandma did the best she could to keep Grandpa in touch with life back in Roseburg. She went to the photo studio often and took many snapshots of herself during her pregnancy. She also sent lots of baby pictures after my dad was born. Some of them said, "Love, from Richard."

Left: Berendt Kappedal with sons Richard (left) and Berendt Jr. Above: Earlamae and Richard

I'm sure that Grandpa could see what a gem he was getting in Grandma just by looking at the pictures. She was quite a whiz with the sewing machine and sewed most of their outfits. Not only that, Grandma was a looker!

After serving almost a year in the Pacific, Grandpa was sent back to Oregon. He finished the rest of his stint in the military and then moved his little family back to northern Minnesota. They farmed there for the rest of their lives and had five more children.

Now, years later, the pictures tell it all! ❖

We Regret to Inform You ...

By Anne Beckwith Johnson

Hand-delivered telegrams in 1944 meant bad news, so when the Western Union man stood at our door that November afternoon, holding a telegram in his hand, he seemed reluctant to give it to me. I looked at the envelope in my hands and saw a row of purple stars stamped above my father-in-law's name in the cellophane window. I had heard that only death notices bore these stars. My vision blurred, and I couldn't breathe.

My mother-in-law came into the hallway. At the sight of the yellow envelope, she gave a faint gasp and paled. We joined my father-in-law in the living room. He slowly opened the envelope and read it aloud, "We regret to inform you ..."

My husband, Vernon, a Flying Fortress pilot, had been flying bombing runs out of Foggia, Italy, over Germany and Austria for two months. I was living in Santa Barbara with his parents and our two baby daughters. His mother, Grace, worried constantly about their only son, but I, with youthful optimism, felt that nothing could happen to my all-powerful 24-year-old husband. We had been married for three years, since I was 17.

The yellow telegram with those threatening purple stars arrived ...

Our first daughter was born a few days after Vernon had been called to preflight. For a year and a half, as he moved through six-week-long pilot-training periods in a variety of godforsaken desert bases, we had followed, living in cheap motels or an overpriced room in someone's home. Once I worked as a waitress in an officer's club so that I could live on the base and have the chance to spend a few hours a week with my husband.

I spent hours with the other wives, our conversations filled with military jargon. We heard of occasional plane crashes in training and waited in tense agony for a message that our men were safe.

After Vernon received his wings, he was made a first pilot and assigned a crew. They received months of B-17 training, but eventually the July day arrived when he was ready to go overseas. I said goodbye to him and his nine crew members in Florida and returned to his parents' home to await the birth of our second child. He wasn't allowed to tell me where he was going, but the secret code in a letter told me it was Italy.

Jill was born two months later. I sent him a prewritten telegram that was to have said, "Congratulations! You have a daughter." In error, he received a birthday greeting and puzzled over the unsuitable words, not knowing about Jill's arrival until my letter reached him.

While I was still in the hospital, I read in the paper that a favorite cousin had been killed over Germany. The war had come still closer. Then my mother died when Jill was six weeks old.

Every day at noon, my mother-in-law and I waited on the front porch for the postman to bring a letter from Vernon. He came to feel responsible if he didn't bring us one. Most were one-page V-mail letters—not much news, but proof that Vernon was alive and well. The fact that the letter had been written some 10 days before never changed our faith. It was the moment of receipt that proved his safety, and we were at peace for another day. The most recent letter was always under my pillow at night with his photo. One week after my mother's funeral, the yellow telegram with those threatening purple stars arrived, and I doubt that I was ever a girl again after that moment.

Reluctantly, Vernon's father opened the envelope and read it aloud: "We regret to inform you that your son was slightly injured in action on Nov. 25, 1944." We grabbed the word *slightly* and read it and interpreted it over and over for the entire evening.

We were luckier than many who waited. The day after the telegram, we received a letter from a hospital chaplain who wrote that "one of your husband's legs has been fractured, but he is doing very well."

A week later, Vernon managed to write. I look at that letter now, with the shaky handwriting, and wonder how he managed to cheer us. It would be another month before we would know that one leg had been amputated and the other held together in a cast for future operations. One shoulder had burned to the bone, and the painful, lengthy process of skin grafts had begun. The burns he suffered over most of his body would heal slowly.

The Christmas cards I had sent to his crew came back to me. Seven young men whom I

had known were dead. It would be months, and in part, years before I would hear about that volunteer night mission.

It was their 13th mission. Before they had reached the target, one of the B-17's engines ran

Above: Author Anne Johnson with daughters Christie and newborn Jill, 1944. Below: The remains of the B-27 from which Vernon Johnson somehow escaped. Facing page: A group of fellow graduates from Class 43-K, at a celebration in Salt Lake City. Anne and Vernon Johnson are on the right.

away and started to burn. They dumped their bomb load over the Adriatic and Vernon headed for an emergency field in northern Italy, but there was a crash on the runway, and they were sent on to a tiny auxiliary field nearby.

On their final approach, with little altitude and a second engine glowing red hot, the lights on the landing strip went out. With no other option, Vernon brought the plane down by a faint string of lights. Suddenly, a two-story stone farmhouse appeared in the landing lights. Pulling up as sharply as possible, he cleared the house and crashed on the other side.

Vernon remembered being unable to move, with men screaming and ammunition going off—and then nothing until he recovered consciousness, lying in a pool of burning gas beneath the wing of the large plane. With one arm, he pulled himself away and again lost consciousness.

He came to in a hospital. Two men in the tail had walked away without a scratch. Seven were killed. It was assumed that Vernon had been blown through the side of the plane when the oxygen tank below his seat exploded.

A few days after Christmas, he sent me a letter saying that his left leg had been amputated. I was to tell his mother, if I thought best. What a burden I would have carried if I hadn't told her that day. He apparently thought we could protect her for a short time. The child of her body had been injured, in pain, marred for life—and she could do nothing to protect him. She wept for hours. His father drank away his agony.

I felt only relief that he was alive and improving. I thought back to the evening when we had sat in his car in front of my college boarding-house and he had said, like others, "If I were to lose a limb in the war, I would never come home!" Now, his fight for life was strong.

Vernon was returned to the States after three months and temporarily assigned to a nearby hospital. We were allowed to bring him home for five days, and we carried him upstairs to our room, where we could spend hours just touching, talking and looking at each other and acquainting him with his baby daughters. At first they were afraid of the stranger in their mother's room.

At last, Vernon lay beside me in our bed, his right leg encased in plaster of paris, the left leg gone below the knee. I touched the still-fresh skin graft scars over his back and shoulder. Part of one ear had been burned away, but the burns on his face had healed, leaving only the faint shine of scar tissue. He was down from his normal 180 pounds to 135, but to me, he was complete and unchanged.

The next afternoon, the postman left his enormous leather mail pouch on the kitchen table and joined us in our room to share a bottle of champagne. One of his boys had returned.

Vernon spent another 15 months in a distant hospital for another amputation on his left leg and for long operations to save his right leg. I visited him once in that hospital filled with young amputees, where I found laughter, terrible jokes and camaraderie.

For me it was another year of single parenthood and loneliness, but also of hope. A few emotional scars in each of us would never heal completely, but the war was over, and only healing lay ahead of us.

When my children asked "What did you do in the war, Mommy?" I replied, "I waited." ❖

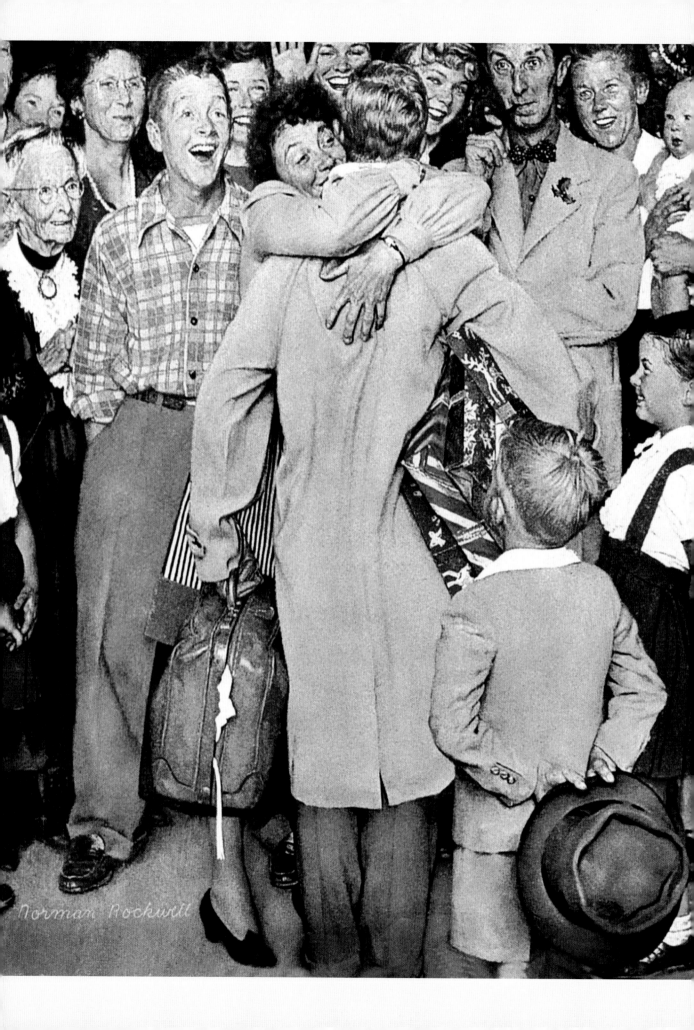

When Johnny Came Marching Home

Chapter Six

By the end of World War II, the home front was worn as thin emotionally as the front lines were physically. When Italy surrendered in September 1943 and then Germany in May 1945, we knew that victory was within grasp. But the months following V-J Day in August 1945 were agonizingly long for many Allied families as they awaited the return of their loved ones.

"Christmas 1945" by Colleen M. Driscoll, published in the December 2003 issue of *Good Old Days* magazine was one poignant snapshot of those bittersweet days:

"It was December 1945. The war in the Pacific was over, and my father was coming home. My mother and I lived in a second-floor flat. We weren't sure if he was going to make it home by Christmas, but we were making preparations in hopes that he would be there soon.

"There were only 10 days left until Christmas, and Mother had gone shopping. When she returned, we would begin decorating the flat. I kept thinking of my father. *Where is he now?*

"The waiting and wondering were almost unbearable, but they paled compared to the joy of knowing that he had made it through the war safely. I remember repeating 'Thank you!' over and over when we got the news that he was on his way home.

"The previous two and a half years of my 8-year-old life were spent worrying and praying. He was on a communications ship with a mine-sweeping convoy, and sometimes he sent me

We weren't sure if my father was going to make it home by Christmas.

letters in Morse code so I could have the fun of deciphering them. The letters came from China, New Guinea and the Philippines, and I watched the mailbox every day, waiting for the next one.

"As I sat on the floor unwrapping green, blue and red ornaments, a funny feeling came over me. I stopped what I was doing and looked up. My eyes opened wide, and I think my mouth fell open. My beloved father had come home.

"I sat for a minute, stunned. Then I jumped up, tears in my eyes, and ran as he appeared in the doorway. I jumped into his arms and we held on to each other, not wanting to let go.

"We went upstairs to talk and wait for Mother. When we heard her coming, we hid so Dad could surprise her. Too late we realized that his Navy hat was on the couch. She walked in the door, spotted the hat and began crying, laughing and gasping, 'Where are you?'

"What a wonderful Christmas we had! I don't remember what presents I got. I just remember that my father and mother were both there. After all these years, I can see him peeking around the door frame as clearly as I did in 1945. That day is etched in my mind, one of the most important days of my life."

This chapter is dedicated to all of those on the home front who waited patiently and faithfully, those who prayed hopefully and fervently, until Johnny came marching home.

—Ken Tate

When Johnny, Joe, Eddie and Adolf Came Marching Home

By Doris Brecka

For all Americans, May 8, 1945, was one of the most important days in our history. Thereafter it would always be known as V-E (Victory in Europe) Day. Coincidentally, it was also the birthday of the new president, Harry S. Truman. Of great additional importance—though mostly to our family and friends—was the fact that it was also our daughter's first birthday. (In time, she would be the oldest of three girls, along with an older brother and a younger one.)

There wasn't a great deal of humor to be found during postwar days. But while it wasn't exactly hilarious, we still can't resist a smile when we remember the time, while sugar rationing was still in force, that our curious little toddler got ahold of the last of the month's quota of red sugar stamps—and promptly chewed and swallowed them.

In turn, their tours of duty came to an end after they served for a total of 23 years.

The oldest boy in our family, Tony, was one of 12 children—six girls and six boys. He and the next oldest son, Charlie, were farmers, and received deferments dependent on production on their dairy farms. The other four boys had been inducted into the Armed Forces, three in the Army and one in the Navy. In turn, their tours of duty came to an end after they served for a total of 23 years—six for John, four for Joe, three for Eddie and 10 for Adolf.

We were thankful to have not only "Johnny come marching home," but his three brothers as well. John had participated in some of the fiercest engagements of the war, taking part in the Battle of the Bulge and serving in a regiment that swam the Rhine River under fire. He was awarded a Purple Heart for his wounds.

Eddie had served on an aircraft carrier in the Pacific. He took part in the assaults on Iwo Jima, Okinawa, Luzon and other Philippine Islands. Our brother Joe spent two years in Trinidad and other foreign locations. Adolf had chosen an extended tour, and he served in Central Europe (extensively in Germany) as well as Korea and Japan.

During the war, we looked forward to the day when we would no longer have to rely on long-awaited leaves and furloughs to keep up our spirits and especially those of our Czecho-slovakian-born parents. Each of those home-comings was an occasion that called for all who could attend. The food was plentiful, especially the fresh supply of Mama Rosa's delicious sweet rolls filled with prune and poppyseed filling, as was the tradition. And of course, there was Papa Anton's dandelion wine, saved for just such an occasion.

There was much gay singing of Old Country folk songs, taught by our parents, inter-spersed with American favorites. There also was enthusiastic dancing of Bohemian polkas far into the night!

It was sad to see each one leave again for an uncertain future, but there was always the hope that it might soon be over.

Eventually V-E Day did come, in May, and at last, in summer, we celebrated V-J (Victory in Japan) Day. To the joy of all of us, the boys came back, one by one. This brought Mama great relief and happiness, even though Papa Anton was gone, having passed away suddenly in December 1944.

Now thoughts began to look to the future. The youngest son brought a bride home from Germany. Two others met and courted local girls and were married within several years. Seven tiny infants were added to the extended fam-ily in the decade following the war. The fourth serviceman returned to our hometown and was once again free to spend much time hunting and fishing in his beloved northern Wisconsin.

Mama Rosa, now many times a grandma, was happy each Sunday to have her modest home overflowing with children and grandchil-dren. From the days when Anton had a butcher shop, she always had a huge kettle on the stove with soup bones simmering away, awaiting the addition of vegetables, noodles, or sauerkraut and dumplings. Her pantry was never without cottage cheese or peach pies. And each Satur-day, there was fresh kolache.

For all the family—but especially for John-ny, Joe, Eddie and Adolf—these well could have been the best years of their lives! ❖

The Greatest Show

By Donald F. Myers

I was 11 years old in August 1945 when the Japanese agreed to surrender terms given by the United States and its Allies.

During the war, troop trains heading through Indianapolis stopped to take on water near my home. As a special project, the Cub Scouts in my den met these troop trains to give the servicemen Kool-Aid, cookies and other comfort items made by our mothers.

The little railway station abutted a 100-acre field owned by Pennsylvania Railroad; all of us in Indy called it Pensy Field. In an effort to keep up civilian morale, traveling circuses were permitted to continue opera-tions during the war. "The Greatest Show on Earth," the Ringling Brothers, Barnum and Bailey Circus, was in Indianapolis and set up on Pensy Field that August day.

The noon matinee had just ended when two long troop trains carrying more than a thousand soldiers pulled onto the siding next to the water tank. About a dozen Cub Scouts and neighborhood kids waited for the sol-diers to disembark. The soldiers were happy to see us kids and clustered around to get their share of the goodies we had.

A few minutes later, three men in civilian attire walked up the embankment. An older man with steel-gray hair asked who was in charge of the troop trains. Fingers pointed to the front of the first train, where the engine was taking on water. The civilians walked to the Pullman serving as the command-post car, where the higher-ranking officers rode.

Not long thereafter, sergeants began pass-ing the word among the troops that Ringling Brothers was putting on a special show just for them, with all the popcorn, peanuts and Coca-Cola they could handle, free of charge.

A cheering roar went up and a thousand soldiers charged across the tracks toward the Big Top. And they took with them a dozen Cub Scouts and other kids to help celebrate V-J Day, thanks to John Ringling North. ❖

When the War Ended

By Linda Williams

I was only 18 months old when Pearl Harbor was bombed, but I still remember the talk of war that rumbled around our old farmhouse until my fifth birthday. That my father might go to war was never a concern. He was a farmer and badly needed on the home front. He even got extra tokens (they looked like blue and red pennies) to be used for gas. When he received more than he needed for gas, he gave the extras to Mom to trade for sugar or shoes.

Wartime memories often emerge from deep, hidden corners of my mind. In later years, when my own two children wanted to know what flavors of ice cream were available, I would tell them of the war days, when vanilla was the only choice.

I also remember the Christmas when, all up and down the hills of our farming community, there was talk of a blackout. Although I was barely old enough to understand the word, I knew that it would mean no Christmas lights. It never came, but a child finds the possibility a worry of huge magnitude.

I had cousins who had left for the front lines. Once, one of them visited our house while on leave. Mother apologized for asking him to sleep on the couch. "Don't worry," he said. "After a foxhole, I could sleep on the ironing board."

My mother worried about the war constantly; she was just that way. She read newspapers, *Life* magazine, and listened faithfully to Walter Winchell on the big living-room radio.

Then, one warm spring afternoon, as I was playing hopscotch on the front walk, my mother burst out the door, screaming with joy. "Europe has surrendered!" she shouted, so loud my father came running from his milking chores.

I didn't know what it all meant, but since I had not seen so much happiness on my mother's face in a long time, it made me happy too.

The summer wore on, and there was still talk of the war that continued to rage in Japan. Our hired hand wore a worried look those days. His 18th birthday was approaching, and so was his call to bear arms for his country.

My father raised a large crop of tomatoes that year, and sold it to the nearby Green Giant Cannery. A group of teenagers came to pick, and each received a bonus of a half-pint of ice cream.

Then, before the sun set on those long summer evenings, my parents would go back to the field to pick more tomatoes. They always took me along, placing me on a stool in a corner of the field, surrounded by my favorite toys.

Suddenly, the church bells from the nearby village began to chime.

I still vividly remember the night the war ended. A hot and humid breeze was attempting to cool off a scorching August day. The spicy scent of freshly picked tomatoes filled the air. Only the occasional mooing of a cow in a nearby field, a deep growl from my collie and the murmurings of my parents as they worked interrupted the silence. It was a serene setting, typical of this rural Pennsylvania countryside.

Church bells from the nearby village began to chime, a sound never heard except on Sunday morning. They echoed through the valley and across the hills to the tomato field.

Loud horns from the few cars on the road in front of the farm began blowing. Joining in the chorus was the horn of our old truck, which had just turned in the lane. My father had loaned the truck to our hired hand, and he was coming to share the news: The war had ended!

Picked tomatoes were hastily loaded on the back of the truck; our hired hand couldn't stop smiling. Work ceased, and we returned to the house for the leftover ice cream and a celebration.

It was the kind of joy that even a 5-year-old could share, and one that I've carried with me for a lifetime. ❖

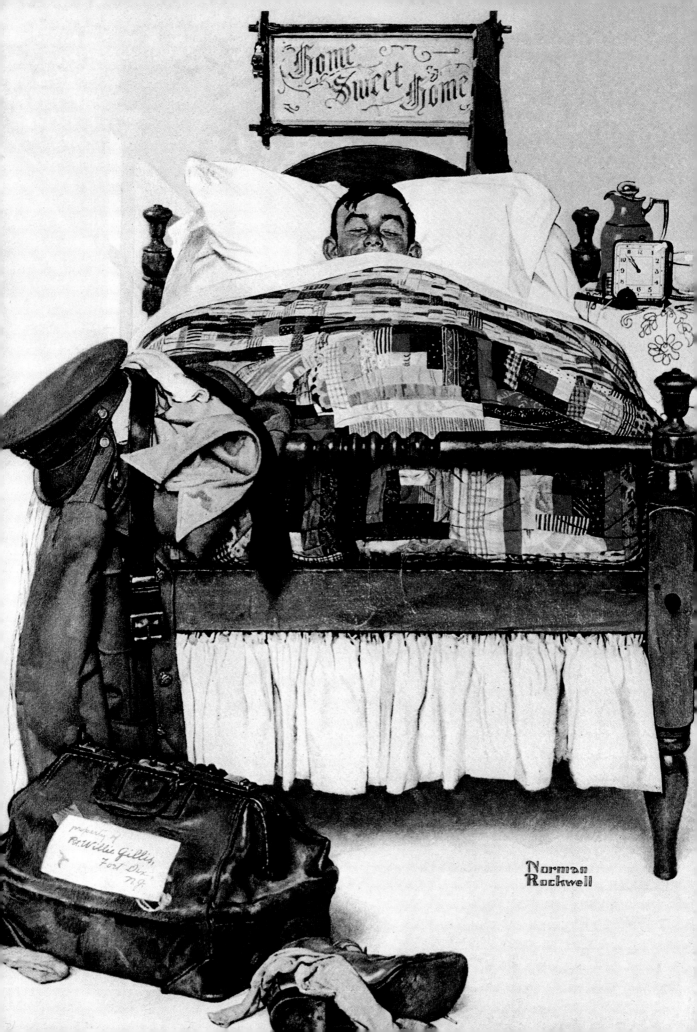

Far, Far Away

By Wilba Lee Featherstone

That long-ago summer of 1943 on my father's farm in the Tennessee hills, I turned 8 years old. As were all my childhood summers, the lazy days were spent roaming the hills and hollows with my brother Edd. But that summer was to be different, for I had become aware of the war. Until that summer, war was only something my parents talked about while they sat listening to the radio—something happening somewhere else, something unreal and far removed from our peaceful green hills.

Edd was five years older than I and knew all about the war. He said it was the reason for the rationing of sugar and coffee and gasoline, and the reason why our brother Ben was somewhere on a ship in the far Pacific. Edd wasn't old enough to go to war, but he did his part. He nailed a picture of Hitler to the smokehouse door and shot it full of holes with his slingshot.

Every day, Edd and I waited beside the mailbox in front of our house.

Daddy worked in Pulaski, a small town 16 miles away, and we received more news of the war than our neighbors did. No one in our part of the hills had electricity, but we owned a battery radio. Sometimes the neighbors would come over at night to listen to the latest news. The adults huddled around the radio while we children chased each other in the cool summer dusk and caught lightning bugs.

Every family on the hill seemed to have someone in the war. I overheard Mother tell Daddy that she hoped the war would be over before her other two sons had to go. I hoped so too. Having no brothers around would be almost as bad as having no sugar for sweetening!

As the summer wore on, the war came closer to home as the radio told of our ships being sunk, our planes being shot down, and our men dying or being taken to prison camps. The papers showed the bloody battlefields, tired and war-worn soldiers, and men who would never again return to the hills.

Ben had not been home in a long time, and we had not heard from him in a long time. Every day, Edd and I waited beside the mailbox in front of our house for the mailman to come. And every day, his old, dust-covered car passed us by.

We would trudge back to the house, dreading the ordeal of telling Mother that again no letter had come, dreading seeing the way her face sagged with sorrow. I remembered how she tried to hide her tears, pretending she had some important chore to do. Sometimes she snatched an old straw hat from a nail on the porch and rushed out to hoe her garden. Sometimes she poured milk into a churn and sat there with the Bible open on her lap, churning and reading, a worried expression on her face.

About every two weeks, Daddy took Mother and Edd and me to Pulaski on Saturday night to hear the high school band play on the square. We stood in the shadows of the old courthouse, munching popcorn and listening to the band play patriotic songs, the chill night air and the music sending shivers along our spines. When they played *Anchors Aweigh,* a lump would rise in my throat, for it was Ben's song—*our* song—and I could see the sailors sailing bravely into battle, the way they had on the screen at the picture show one Saturday night.

Summer passed and autumn came. The green hills turned from red and gold, but still no letter came from Ben. I now realized what the word *war* meant. It meant goodbyes, crying, missing, sadness and dying.

Mother cried often, no longer trying to hide her tears, and Daddy's face became sad and drawn. Edd and I still waited for the mailman. In fact, our whole life seemed to center on that dusty old car and the good news we hoped it would bring.

Then, one evening, Daddy came home early from work, and as we sat down to supper, a smile suddenly flitted across his thin lips. His usually stern voice was soft and kind as he told us that he had received a telegram from Ben, and he was on his way home.

The following days were full and happy as Mother bustled around the kitchen, singing—something she hadn't done for a long time—and baking all the things Ben liked best. She used the sugar she had been hoarding to bake a big chocolate cake and several pies. When Daddy came home at night,

Above: Ben and Daddy.
Below: The author and Edd were more often than not disappointed when they waited at the mailbox for a V-mail letter, such as this one, from their brother.

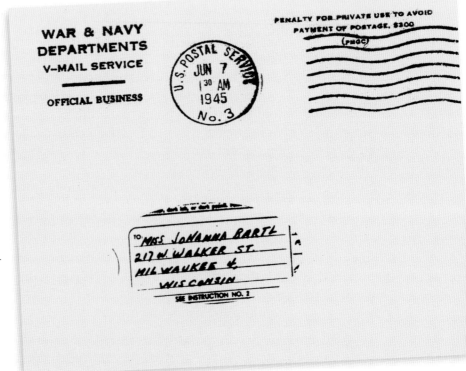

he no longer sat staring into space while he listened to the latest news, but sat placidly reading his paper, the worry lines gone from his weathered face.

I remember the night we went to Pulaski to meet Ben's train. The station was closed and deserted at that late hour. Daddy, Mother, Edd and I stood in the chilly autumn night, waiting, our happiness enfolding us like a warm woolen cape. A yellow lightbulb spotted with dead insects hung above the station platform,

The author, Wilba Lee, found out what war really meant.

casting an eerie glow across the railroad tracks. Edd and I pretended we were tightrope walkers as we balanced our bare feet on the narrow steel rails. Somewhere up the street, a church was holding its fall revival, and now and then, the congregation would lift their voices in song and prayer.

Suddenly the night was alive with a rumbling that grew louder and louder, and the tracks started to shake as though a gigantic monster were hurrying toward us. Mother pulled Edd and me close to her and tried to sound stern as she warned us not to get in front of the train, but her voice trembled with excitement.

The train was now upon us, roaring and pounding, its bright light shining, its whistle screaming across the night. I thought for a moment that it was going on by, it took so long to stop.

We walked close to the cars, straining to see into the dimly lit interior, searching for Ben's familiar face. We watched the doors for someone to get off, but no one did. Only a tired-looking conductor waved to us as the train started to move again. I looked up into Mother's face and read the disappointment written there, the disappointment I was feeling, the disappointment I knew Edd and Daddy felt.

The big engine coughed and wheezed, picking up speed as it moved away down the track, but still we stood, unable to move or speak. There would be no more trains until morning, and tomorrow maybe it would be the same, waiting and nobody coming—like the mailman and the letters that never came.

Then we turned at the sound of footsteps, and from out of the darkness, a smiling sailor appeared. Always one for surprises, Ben had slipped off the train farther down the track.

With a cry of joy, I ran to him, and he dropped his bag and scooped me up in his arms. Then Mother was there, hugging him and crying, and Daddy kept clearing his throat as if a cinder from the train had lodged in it, while Edd stood grinning and wiping his eyes on his sleeve.

We were all trying to talk at once as we piled into Daddy's pickup truck and headed for home. Edd and I rode in the truck bed, huddled near the cab, trying to hear what was being said inside, but all we heard was the happy murmur of voices, and in the distance, the lonesome wail of a train.

We snuggled down into an old ragged quilt that Daddy kept in the truck and wondered if Ben had brought us a souvenir from across the sea, and if we would ever get to ride on a train. The dark tree branches waved to us as we sped through the night, and the swift wind seemed to call: "Ben is home! Ben is home!" as it danced down the road, gathering dust and scattering it across the houses and trees. Once more, the hills were peaceful and still; once more, the war was far, far away. ❖

Norman Rockwell

Celebrating the End

By Doug Glant

I have recollections of things that might have happened before I was 2, but I won't bet on their accuracy. But the first memory I am sure of, from May 7, 1945, is still vivid. And it is the only memory I have of World War II. It was a warm spring day in Seattle, and Mr. Friedhoff, my grandparents' kindly old German gardener, was working in the small front yard.

The backyard, which gently rolled toward the banks of Portage Bay, an offshoot of Lake Washington, was much larger, a many-hued garden of flowers and fruit trees with a vine-covered white lattice arbor.

Mr. Friedhoff had been one of Seattle's most popular landscape specialists before the war, but he had been reduced to simple and less rewarding tasks after Dec. 7, 1941. He had lived in the United States since 1920 and was quite a patriot.

He was especially proud of his two sons in the U.S. Army, one of whom had been wounded at Anzio. But his heavy Teutonic accent had proven distasteful to most of his clientele. My Jewish grandparents, however, thought it absurd to punish him for the Nazis' crimes.

> *I had never seen an adult cry before. I repeated, "Thank God, the war is over."*

I suspect I was more of an encumbrance than an aid, but Mr. Friedhoff always seemed to enjoy my attempts to help him with the gardening.

He always lovingly set me to small tasks—digging at a weed, planting a bulb, disposing of grass cuttings (though I usually created an even larger mess).

Sometimes I got him a glass of water or lemonade, which, in spite of Nana's admonitions, I was adept at spilling. But he would chuckle and give me reassuring pats and words. He was my favorite "uncle." I especially enjoyed the times when he took his lunch break and regaled me with stories of his youth in the Old Country, before automobiles, before World War I, and before someone called Hitler, whose name he spat out as if it were almost unspeakably vile.

He knew the name of every plant and flower in the garden and patiently pointed them out to me. He was as gentle with the vegetation as he was with me. His hands were huge and heavily callused, but he handled even the hardiest of plants with delicacy.

"That's a plum tree, Duckie. That's apple. Those are roses. The pretty vild ones are trillium. Gott blesses us with all this beauty, and we have to take gute care of it."

On this sunny morning, Nana and Papa seemed quite excited about something they heard on the radio. I didn't know it at the time, but they were listening to the scratchy sounds of Gen. Dwight David Eisenhower as he announced the unconditional surrender of Nazi Germany less than a month after Franklin Roosevelt's death and Adolph Hitler's suicide.

My beloved grandparents embraced each other for a very long time. Then they hugged me. They rarely used the front door, but now they flung it open and pointed to Mr. Friedhoff, who was trimming the small strip of lawn that bordered the sidewalk.

"Dougie, go tell Mr. Friedhoff, 'Thank God the war is over.'" I didn't know what that meant, but I did as they asked.

Mr. Friedhoff put down his trimmer and looked at me, his dark eyes filling with tears. "Vhat did you say, Duckie?"

I was a little frightened; I had never seen an adult cry before. But I repeated, "Thank God, the war is over."

Then the large man with the weathered, whiskery face and enormous hands did something that shocked me. He picked me up and sobbed into my neck, kissing me, stroking my head, and babbling over and over again, "Yes, thank Gott, the war is over."

My cheeks were wet with his tears, but I was no longer scared, for I could see the reassuringly sweet looks on my grandparents' faces. They, too, were crying quietly. I knew something good had happened, but why were they crying? It was many years later that I learned about tears of joy.

We went down to the Olympic Hotel that afternoon to join the throng of happy people who were celebrating in Victory Square on University Street, which had been closed off since the war began. And though I still can picture the jubilant crowd, that has never been as powerful as the memory of dear old Mr. Friedhoff and the unplumbable depths of my grandparents' goodness. ❖

Above: The author at age 2 or 3.
Below: From left to right: Jules Glant (Papa), Ethel Glant (Nana), Great-Aunt Belle Woods, and Kurt Friedhoff.

It's Over!

By Robert Gaskill

As a 15-year-old, I was at that questionable age where some things left more of a lasting impression than others. I remember 1945 as a year of major happenings, beginning with the death of President Roosevelt on April 12, at Warm Springs, Ga., and the surrender of Germany on May 7. The first atomic bomb was dropped on Hiroshima, Japan, on Aug. 6, and the second bomb on Nagasaki on Aug. 9.

Aug. 15, 7 p.m.: We had just finished supper, and Mom and Dad were clearing the dining-room table. The old Emerson table-model radio in the kitchen was playing the standard popular music of the day.

We all came to an abrupt halt when the radio announcer said, "We interrupt this program to bring you an important war bulletin. The White House in Washington has just released the following statement: The Japanese have accepted our terms of surrender fully and completely; this means that this is the end of the Second World War."

Lines of servicemen watch as General MacArthur signs as supreme allied commander during formal surrender ceremonies on the USS *Missouri* in Tokyo Bay.

Everybody in every neighborhood in the whole world must have been listening to that particular broadcast because everywhere I could see, doors opened with a bang and the biggest party the world has ever seen began.

The streets filled with throngs of people. Car horns sounded, and people yelled and screamed out the news to those who had not yet heard.

Pushing my way down Fifth Street in the middle of the trolley-car tracks, I made my way to Chew Street, where the gang was. Pavie, Kimmel, Pfeifle, Kraft and Ziggy stood in the middle of the trolley-car tracks, shouting the news to the people on the car.

The trolley that traversed between Center City (Philadelphia) and Godfrey Avenue was bogged down in a sea of screaming people who for four long years mostly had kept silent about everything good or bad. We were all in the same boat. Nobody wanted to hear your bad news—and the good news you kind of kept to yourself, realizing that not everybody was as fortunate.

People emerged from the trolley to join the crowd pressing around them. I don't think any of them even cared if they got home that night. They were swallowed up by the masses.

Somewhere in the distance I heard the faint sounds of an accordion. I decided to head for it. I finally got down to the Colney Theater, and standing out in front was my good friend Stan, playing his heart out with *I'll Be Seeing You.* On the second chorus, everybody sang along.

Stan, who was about 27, worked at Steinway Piano. He played every instrument made and did a lot of acting as an extra on radio stations in the Philadelphia area. Stan saw me in the crowd, nodded and smiled. I went over and told him to play *Pennsylvania Polka* next. The people made room where none had existed. Before the song was over, half the street was doing the polka. Stan was on his way to the best gig he ever played.

Meanwhile, I headed down Fifth Street. Coming up to the Sun Ray Drug Store on the corner, I heard a portable radio relaying the latest news. A large crowd had gathered to listen. The newscaster was repeating the news we had all heard, but everyone listened because they just wanted to be sure it was all true.

I started back toward home, finding the center of the street to be the easiest way to go. Mr. Gettlin, who operated the local record store and lived on the second floor, was hanging a speaker out the window to play music for those below. Stan was still belting it out in front of the Colney Theater, and I guessed he was in for a long night.

With the music fading in the background, I crossed Chew Street past the deserted trolley car. My friends Jack and Don were sitting on it, taking in the whole scene.

Evening came. Stores and houses turned their lights on. Dim-outs and blackouts were in the past. I heard fireworks from side streets.

And so went this outpouring of emotion that had been held in our minds for four long years. The victories we had won on the battlefields of the world had been stored in our brains in alphabetical order with a "hold" notice to celebrate each of them when, collectively, they would finally bring about the end of the war.

Everyone celebrated. People I hadn't seen for months suddenly were part of the scene, shaking hands with anybody they could. Even the grouchy old lady who always called the cops on us when we played street football near her house was in the middle of the street, laughing and talking to everyone—including the kids she didn't like.

Doors opened and the biggest party the world has ever seen began.

As I made my way back up Fifth Street, finding it hard to pass anyone without shaking hands or wishing them well, I noticed the lone figure of Mrs. Dorman standing on her front porch, just looking over the whole scene. Tears streamed down her face as she cried uncontrollably. Mrs. Dorman had just recently received her official status as a Gold Star Mother. She had lost a son in the war. He was killed while attempting to land his crippled bomber, after first having his crew bail out—a hero's death.

Jubilation left me. I pushed through the crowd and walked up to Mrs. Dorman. She met me on the top step, put her arms around me and wept in convulsive sobs. She finally pushed herself away, but with her hands still on my shoulders, she said, "Thank you for coming up, Bob. I feel better now." She turned, opened the door with the Gold Star on it, and disappeared inside.

I stood there for a long time, wiping tears off my cheeks. As I left the porch, the happiness of the crowds was no longer so important. The shouting and laughter now seemed to be coming from the end of a long, dark tunnel, and the noise was very faint. Mrs. Dorman must have touched my soul that day. I've never felt like that, before or since. ❖

Victory and Castanets

By Jo Ann Armstrong

*I*n August 1945, I lived with my family in a small town on the Hudson River. Many people there still remember the day World War II ended, but I was only 5 years old that summer, and my memories are those of a little girl. Although I had a limited understanding of what was happening at the time, I sensed it was something important, and I felt the excitement.

As I recall, the domed wooden radio in the living room had been turned on early that special morning, and it blared so loudly that I could hear it on the front porch where I sat waiting for the iceman. We had a refrigerator, but the families in the apartment building across the street still had iceboxes.

When the iceman finally came, he was in such a good mood that he chopped great chunks from a huge cake of ice, and then gave them to the children who always hung around his truck. It was an unusual gesture for him; normally, he only gave us a little sliver. Today, however, he was feeling generous.

The next recollection I have is of the fire whistle howling from the high tower in the middle of town and of our black-and-white terrier, Nipper, wailing right along with it. I thought she would never stop. We named her after the RCA dog, and we often wondered, from the way she tilted her head toward the radio while it was playing, if she believed that was who she was.

The next thing I remember I was in the drugstore with my teenage sister. It was packed with people hugging and talking exuberantly. Many held their fingers up in the "V for victory" sign. I sat at the counter and tried to drink a vanilla phosphate, as I often did, but with all the excitement going on, that phosphate was the farthest thing from my mind. Everyone was so elated that they just kept chattering and laughing, and saying the boys would be home soon. The war had ended.

I looked around at all the happy faces and saw a woman standing alone, away from the crowd. She was so quiet. Then she noticed me watching her, and as she walked toward me, she took a white, red-bordered pin with three blue stars in the center from her collar. It looked just like the banner I had seen in her window.

She handed the pin to me. "I want you to have this so you will always remember the day the war ended. I'll miss it, but I know you'll take good care of it, won't you?" Later I learned that the stars represented three men from her family who were in the armed services. The pins, the size of the small battle ribbons worn by servicemen who had seen action, were proudly worn by people who had immediate family members in the service of their country.

My sister kept telling me Uncle Midge would be coming home, and I thought I would burst with joy at the news. He was one of my favorite people—and not just because he always brought me presents, either.

Finally, it was night, and the best part began. There was a dilapidated old diner on Main Street that had stood empty for years. Someone decided it was all right to rip it down and burn it, and that's exactly what happened—right in the middle of the road where the four corners met.

The fire engines arrived and the men hooked up the hose. Then someone lit a fire. I can still see people tearing apart that old building and tossing the scraps of lumber onto the blaze until it became a roaring bonfire. It was like some ancient ritual performed by a primitive tribe.

When the last of Maggie's Diner was in flames, everyone started singing and dancing around it. Then he was there—the man with the castanets. I had never gotten a good look at him before, but on warm Saturday evenings when the doors to the Irish pub down the street were thrown open, I could hear his castanets clicking away as people sang and cheered him on.

I inched my way over to this mysterious

This "in-service flag" is an example of those given to families with loved ones serving in World War II. The pin given to the author on V-J Day in 1945 was modeled after such a flag. A blue star was sewn onto the flag for each family member serving in the Armed Forces. A gold star sewn atop a blue one indicated a family member who was killed in action. Photo courtesy the National Archives.

man until I was so close that I could look up at his intense face with its silver-gray walrus mustache and aquamarine eyes. He was stooped and old, but his white hair was thick and bushy, and he moved like a young man. I stood there for a long time, entranced, watching him play.

His fingers fluttered like hummingbirds' wings, and as a crowd sang, he picked up the tunes, clicking them out with his magic clappers. I looked over once or twice to see my sister having a wonderful time, her black hair shining in the firelight. But mainly, I watched him play those castanets.

When the flames died out, the fire company hosed down the area and the people left, still singing and laughing. The old man was the last to go.

Awhile later, my Uncle Midge came home and brought me a present. It was a wooden MacArthur doll dressed in a khaki uniform and wearing a general's cap with fancy gold trim. I felt so unhappy that I cried because it wasn't a beautiful little girl doll with a pretty dress. That's when he gave me the silver dollar. I've kept it all these years—along with the pin—in my special memory box.

The doll has long ago gone to doll heaven, but every so often, I hold in my hand the mementos so highly regarded by a little girl. Then I think of Uncle Midge and the doll—and Nipper—and the night the war ended! ❖

Victory and the Fire Bell

By Venus E. Bardanouve

Word of the Japanese surrender spread through the town that hot August day of 1945. We could hardly believe it could be true, but the radio kept proclaiming the news of victory. I remember my own sense of unbelief. Could it really be? Was the war finally over?

I was staying with my parents in the little town of St. Paul, Neb., while my sailor husband was on the West Coast, awaiting orders to go to sea.

He had been in the service for almost four years, and it was hard to realize that now life could return to normal.

The people of the town seemed to need to be together on this momentous occasion. They left their houses and gathered in neighboring yards, sharing the news. Then they began to congregate on the town's main street, milling around and talking about the surrender.

They seemed more subdued and dazed than jubilant. Many had blue stars in their windows indicating they had someone in the service. Blue stars had been replaced by gold ones in honor of men and women who would not return.

I remember thinking that there should be a band playing, someone making a rousing victory speech, fireworks or something dazzling to help us realize that the news was really true!

We wanted to celebrate, but we were unsure what to do. Then one of the men looked at the nearby fire station bell tower and shouted, "Let's ring the bell!" The spell was broken, and everyone rushed to gather at the foot of the steel tower. That was what we needed to ring out the victory! He then spotted me standing there,

Left: The author's husband and Kathie's father, Herb Cecil.
Right: The author's daughter, Kathie, in her sailor dress.

holding the hand of my 4-year-old daughter who was wearing her sailor dress.

"There's a serviceman's family!" he shouted. "Let's let little Kathie Cecil ring the bell!"

He picked up my lovely little daughter and helped her pull the bell rope. Over and over it pealed. The spell was broken, and the people began to cheer. Tears ran down faces. Some were tears of relief that their servicemen and women were safe now and surely would soon be home. Other tears were for those families whose loved ones would never return.

One young man from our town had been on the Bataan march and had died in a Japanese camp. Another had been lost at Pearl Harbor. Others died or were wounded on battlefields or at sea around the world.

But underneath all the emotions—the cheers and tears—was the pealing of the firehouse bell proclaiming to our little part of the world that freedom for all was worth fighting for, and now peace could once again fill the land! And a little girl in a sailor dress helped us all celebrate the victory. ❖